PSALMS FR

3.95

Psalms from Taizé

Companion Volume to

PRAISE IN ALL OUR DAYS

MOWBRAY
LONDON & OXFORD

ISBN 0 264 66918 5

This edition first published in England 1983
by A. R. Mowbray & Co. Ltd.,
Saint Thomas House, Becket Street,
Oxford, OX1 1SJ

Phototypeset by Cotswold Typesetting Ltd., Gloucester
Printed in Great Britain by Spottiswoode Ballantyne Ltd.

CONTENTS

INTRODUCTION

If the two main expressions of Christian prayer are thought of as 'Alleluia' and 'Kyrie Eleison', then the Psalms are the highest interpretation of those two cries. The cry of joy in God, Creator and Saviour; the cry to God in times of anguish, both personal and collective.

Needless to say, the Psalms are not all of equal beauty, and there are a certain number that we find it impossible to sing with our modern hearts, even if they remain part of God's Word to us.

So in Taizé we use a selection of the Psalms, and often at any one service we only sing one portion of one Psalm, in order to savour it to the full.

It is our hope that this Psalter, made for use by brothers living in English-speaking countries, may help others to praise God in 'Psalms and Hymns and Spiritual Songs'.

Psalm Numbering

The **bold numbers** of the Psalms follow the order of the Greek Septuagint, Catholic and Orthodox liturgical numbering. In most Bibles, the Hebrew numbering is used; this is also the Anglican liturgical numbering (*shown in italic*).

Sept. **9B** =*Heb.10*
Sept. **10** =*Heb. 11* etc.
Sept. **113A**=*Heb. 114*
Sept. **113B**=*Heb. 115*
Sept. **114** =*Heb. 116A*
Sept. **115** =*Heb. 116B*
Sept. **116** =*Heb. 117* etc.
Sept. **146** =*Heb. 147A*
Sept. **147** =*Heb. 147B*

Doxologies

A. All gl*o*ry to the F*a*ther on h*i*gh,
to his S*o*n Jesus Chr*i*st, the L*o*rd,
to the Sp*i*rit who dw*e*lls in our h*ea*rts,
both n*o*w and for *e*ver. Am*e*n.

B. All gl*o*ry to the F*a*ther on h*i*gh,
to his S*o*n, Jesus Chr*i*st,
to the Sp*i*rit who dw*e*lls in our h*ea*rts.
both n*o*w and everm*o*re.

A. is used for most Psalms.
B. is used for Psalms alternating 3 and 2 stress lines.

NB. When using the 'simple formulae', A is always employed.

Psalms from Taizé

Psalm 1 *(Heb. 1)*

Antiphon: The Lord will bless us,
if we walk in the way of peace.

How happy is the man, how bless'd,
who refuses the counsels of the doomed,
not passing where the sinful pass,
nor sitting with the foolish who mock,
but his delight is the Law of the Lord,
and he ponders it, night and day.

He is like a tree which is set
on the edge of a flowing stream;
he gives fruit when the season comes,
on his branches, no wilting leaves;
all that he does goes well,
not so the wicked, not so!

They are like straws in the wind,
borne away without trace;
when judged, unable to stand
or join with those who are true;
the Lord is the guide of the just
but the wicked man's way leads to doom.

Psalm 2 *(Heb. 2)*

Antiphon: The Lord has set his Son upon a throne on high.

Why do the nations rebel?
What folly all their peoples speak!
The kings of the earth stand up,
the rulers conspire against God
  —against his king!
'How long must we carry their bonds?
Come, let us throw off their yoke.'

The Lord reigns and sees from on high,
he laughs and puts them to scorn;
for then in his wrath he speaks,
and his fury fills them with dread—
'It is I who have set my king
on Zion, my holy hill.'

The Lord has said: You are my Son,
begotten by me this day;
only ask, and all the nations are yours,
to the uttermost ends of the earth;
yours to inherit and to rule,
to shatter with a sceptre of steel.

Kings, pay heed to my words,
take note, rulers of the world;
come, serve the Lord with awe,
tremble before him, bow low;
for if ever his fury should blaze,
your lives will come to an end.

Psalm 3 *(Heb. 3)*

Antiphon: Lord, give your people your joy.

——

So many my enemies, O Lord!
So many rise up against me,
so many voices proclaim:
No salvation for him in his God.

But you are my Glory and my Shield,
my God, you lift up my head;
I cry out, I call to the Lord,
from his holy height he replies.

I lie down and I take my rest,
then I wake, for the Lord is my guard;
I am not afraid, though vast crowds
stand against me on every side.

Stand up, O Lord, now and save me,
Lord, give your people your joy.

Psalm 4 *(Heb. 4)*

Antiphon: In the night, I can take my rest,
you alone keep my life secure.

When I call, you give heed, O Lord, righteous God;
free me from my anguish, pity, hear my prayer.

How long will they all remain hard of heart?
How long will their lies and their vanity endure?

Remember, the Lord does wonders for his friends,
the Lord will hear when I call on his name.

Do not sin but tremble,
as you lie on your bed, in silence reflect,
offer praise and worship, trust in the Lord.

Many sigh as they pray: Lord, show us your joy;
when shall we see the light of your face?

In my heart you have poured the fullness of joy,
far richer than their harvests of corn and wine.

In peace I lie down and sleep comes at once,
for you, Lord, alone, keep my life secure.

Praise the Father, the Son, praise the Holy Spirit,
now and for ever and world without end.

Psalm 5 *(Heb. 5)*

Antiphon: Lord, you bless all who are just,
your kindness surrounds us with good.

———

O Lord, give heed to my words,
listen as I cry;
hear me when I call for help,
my Master and God.

I pray to you, Lord, each day,
you hear me at dawn;
I rise and stand in your sight,
with an eager heart.

You do not approve sinful men,
the proud are not your friends;
the arrogant cannot draw near,
no place in your sight.

But kindly you bring me with love
to the place where you dwell;
I fall down, filled with awe,
and worship your name.

You know all my enemies, O Lord,
show me where to go,
the path where your justice guides.

No, they are not to be trusted,
they will only destroy;
their lips are a gaping tomb,
though their words are so sweet.

But for all whom you defend there is joy,
they will rejoice evermore;
you bless them and give them delight
in your boundless love.

Psalm 6 *(Heb. 6)*

Antiphon: How much longer, O Lord, how long?
Come to my rescue in love.

Do not overwhelm me, O Lord,
do not chastise me in wrath;
have pity on my weakness, O God,
heal my wounded heart,
the anguish deep in my soul.

How much longer, O Lord, how long?
Quickly, save me, return,
come to my rescue in love,
for who recalls in the tomb?
And where are you praised by the dead?

See, I am too weary to sigh,
at night I fall down and weep,
my tears have flooded the night,
for sorrow my eyes are dim,
I grow old, filled with grief.

Now away, all doers of wrong!
For my groaning is dear to the Lord;
he has heard my voice as I called,
he has welcomed my trusting prayer,
my enemies are put to shame,
routed and driven away.

Psalm 8 *(Heb. 8)*

Antiphon: How great is you name, O Lord our God,
how glorious your name!

How great is your name, O Lord our God,
how glorious your name!

Set high over all the earth,
majestic to highest heaven;
you fashion the praises of babes,
you silence the boasts of your foes.

When I see the moon and the stars,
the sky which your hand has formed
—what is man, then, that you love him,
the children of men, that you care?

Less than an angel you made him;
you crowned him with honour and light;
all things created are his
—'Take charge of the world I have made.'

Both sheep and cattle you gave him,
and even the wildest beasts,
birds flying, the fish of the sea,
with all that dwells in the deep.

How great is your name, O Lord our God,
how glorious your name!

Psalm 9 (extract) *(Heb. 9)*

Antiphon: The Lord defends the oppressed,
in trouble he defends the poor.

I will praise you, Lord, with all my heart,
I will tell all the wonders you have done;
I will exult and rejoice, O God,
I will sing and praise your name.

For see, my enemies have fled,
cast down and overawed by your might;
you have sustained my cause,
high-throned, righteous Lord. (. . .)

Eternal is the throne of our God,
on high he prepares to judge;
he comes to the world with right,
with justice he governs the earth.

The Lord defends the oppressed,
in trouble he upholds the poor;
all who know you have trust,
you do not abandon those who seek.

Sing praises to the Lord in Zion,
proclaim all his wonderful deeds;
he remembers the blood that was spilled,
he recalls our cries and our pain. (. . .)

Psalm 10 *(Heb. 11)*

Antiphon: The Lord is just, he loves justice,
the righteous will see his face.

The Lord shall be my refuge,
why do you say to my soul:
'Little bird, fly away to the hills?'

'See, the wicked have drawn their bows,
the arrows are poised on the strings;
they will shoot at the good by night,
who can hope, since the pillars are down?'

But behold the Lord in his splendour,
on high the Lord sits enthroned;
his eyes survey the whole world,
to test and sound every heart.

God knows who is wicked and just,
he rejects every lover of wrong;
on the evil he sends fiery coals,
pouring out storms of flame.

The Lord is just, he loves justice,
the righteous will see his face.

Psalm 12 *(Heb. 13)*

Antiphon: In your goodness, O Lord, I put my trust,
and my heart finds its joy in you.

How long will you forget me, O Lord? Till I die?
How long, O God, will you hide your face?
How long must my soul pine away in grief?
How long will my enemies boast in pride?

God, my God, look down and reply,
give light to my eyes, that they close not in death;
let my rivals not rejoice: at last we have won!
My enemies will laugh if they see me fall.

In your goodness, Lord, I have put my trust,
my heart will rejoice, you are strong to save;
I will praise your love and your kindness, O God,
for ever I will sing for my Lord, the Most High.

Psalm 14 *(Heb. 15)*

Antiphon: O Lord, who can approach you,
or draw near to your holy hill?

O Lord, who can approach you,
or draw near to your holy hill?

The one whose way is with God,
whose paths are justice and right,
whose words are true and sincere,
no trace of slander and lies,

who speaks no ill of his neighbour
and causes his friends no harm,
who honours all who fear God
and is always true to his word;

who will not lend money for gain,
whose judgement cannot be bought;
all who live in this way
will dwell for ever in peace.

Psalm 15 *(Heb. 16)*

Antiphon: Defend me, God, my refuge and shield;
I say to the Lord: You alone are my life.

Defend me, God, my refuge and shield;
I say to the Lord: You alone are my life.

Their 'glory' and 'princes' I know to be in vain,
but more and more their idols abound;
they multiply sorrow and they run after grief,
never will I worship or bow to their shame.

O Lord, my lot, my portion and my cup,
you have promised and you will not fail:
a corner of blessing, marked by the cord,
my delight is a land you have sworn to give.

I will bless the Lord who has guided my course,
in the deep of night I wake up in joy;
I will keep the Lord before me all the day long,
since he is at my right I shall not fall.

My heart rejoices and my soul is glad,
my body too lies quiet at rest;
you will not abandon my soul in hell,
no corruption will your servant see.

You will show me the path of life,
before your face is fullness of joy,
by your side is undying bliss.

Psalm 16 (extract) *(Heb. 17)*

Antiphon: I will go in justice to behold your face,
when I awake, you will fill me with joy.

———

Pay heed, O God, and give justice,
hear me when I cry;
listen to the sound of my prayer,
I will speak no deceit;
you will decide in my favour,
you behold what is right.

You come by night, and you fathom my heart,
you try me but find no shadow of lies,
my tongue has never sinned in the way that men do.

You speak, and I am eager to keep your words,
I follow your paths, those set by your Law;
from your Way, I intend that my feet shall not stray.

I rise and I call, you answer me, Lord,
to my anxious voice you incline your ear:
O gracious Saviour, reveal your great love.

They stand up, and menace my life,
save me, I am dear in your sight,
hide me in the shadow of your wings.

I will go, in justice, to behold your face,
when I awake, you will fill me with joy.

Psalm 17 *(Heb. 18)*

I

Antiphon: In anguish I cried out to the Lord,
from his temple he heard my voice.

I love you, O Lord, my strength,
my Saviour, you have saved me by your power;
the Lord is my rock everlasting,
God is my stronghold and shield.

I take shelter in him, he defends me,
like a wall, he defends me from harm;
my shelter, my fortress, I will praise him,
he saves me when I call upon his name.

The floods of death surged around,
huge waves sweeping over my head;
the snares of hell sprang shut
and death had prepared all her traps.

In anguish, I cried out to the Lord,
I pleaded with God for help;
from his temple he heard my voice,
his ear perceived my call.

And the earth trembled, it shook,
the foundations of the mountains were moved,
he came breathing out smoke and flames,
burning coals proclaimed his approach.

He tore open the heavens, he came down,
with dark clouds stretched under his feet;
his mount was a cherub, he flew
throned high on the wings of the wind.

Deepest night was the veil of his presence,
and thick clouds of rain, his royal tent;
lightning cut through the clouds,
hurling hailstones and billows of fire.

Then God spoke from on high,
the thunder of the Most High pealed;
with his arrows he put them to flight,
by his power they were scattered abroad.

The floor of the sea lay uncovered,
the foundations of the world were bare,
when the Lord spoke, the sea fled,
at the sound of his furious words.

Then the Lord stretched out his hand,
he reached down and saved me from on high;
he pulled me out of the flood,
away from the power of my foes.

They were strong, they attacked in force,
but the Lord was near, my shield;
he brought me through, set me free,
he saved me, for great is his love.

II

Antiphon: You are my lamp, O Lord,
you brighten my darkness away.

———

God rewards me because I am just,
I am pure so he opens his heart;
I have kept the laws of the Lord,
and never turned from my God.

All his commands, I have kept,
and his laws are ever in my sight,
see, I am sinless in his eyes,
he knows, I have done no wrong.

He rewards me because I do right,
before him I am free of guilt;
you are a friend of all friends,
true with all who are true,
pure with those who are pure,
but cunning with the men who deceive,
you save the humble and poor,
all who boast are brought down.

For you are my lamp, O Lord,
you brighten my darkness away;
you give me strength to advance,
with God, I scale every wall.

Our God—how perfect his ways!
All his words are tested and true;
he alone is the shield
of all who seek his help.

Who is God, other than the Lord?
What rock can compare with our God?
He girdles me round with strength,
he keeps me safe in his ways.

He gives me feet agile as a deer's
as I climb from peak to peak;
he trains my hands in warfare,
my arms to bend a bow of steel.

You defend me, God, and you save me,
your love and power are my shield;
you guide my steps, keep me free,
you uphold me, I shall not fall. (. . .)

God lives, praised be my Rock!
Exalt in the Lord who saves!
The victory comes from his hand,
see, my enemies fall in awe.

I am saved from the raging of my foes,
you lift me up, high above their heads;
you defend me from the violence of men,
I will praise you in all the world.

God gives great triumphs to the King,
he reveals to his Chosen One his love,
love for David and his line;
praised be the Lord evermore!

Psalm 18 *(Heb. 19)*

Antiphon: The Word of the Lord is true indeed,
it brings life everlasting.

The heavens proclaim the glory of God,
the firmament declares the work of his hands;
each day repeats the tale to day,
and night confides the knowledge to night.

No word of speech, no sound is heard,
silence is the voice they use,
yet all the earth perceives the news,
their gospel runs to the ends of the world.

On high there is set a dwelling for the sun,
he strides each day like a bridegroom from the door,
rejoicing to begin his triumphant course.

At heaven's end his race begins,
his setting touches the farthest extreme,
and nothing is hid from his scorching beams.

How perfect, the Law of the Lord,
it comforts the heart;
all his commandments are sure,
his wisdom overflows.

The precepts of God are true,
delight of the soul;
how just are all his commands,
the light of our lives.

The worship of God is pure,
for ever it endures;
the judgements of the Lord are just,
both fair and good.

All, more desirable than gold,
  than purest gold;
sweeter than honey, his commands,
  than nectar in the comb.

So your servants learn from your laws,
  to keep them brings great gain;
but who can perceive his own faults?
  Forgive my secret sin.

Preserve your servant from pride,
  let me not be its slave;
then I shall be blameless and pure,
  unstained by any sin.

Accept all the words of my mouth,
  and the thoughts of my heart,
all the days of my life, O Lord,
  my Redeemer, my God.

Psalm 19 *(Heb. 20)*

Antiphon: In days of distress, may the Lord be your help,
may your safety come from the God of Jacob.

In days of distress, may the Lord be your help,
may your safety come from the God of Jacob.

From his sanctuary, may the Lord send you help,
may he send you his aid from Zion,
may he accept the gifts you offer,
be pleased with your sacrifice of praise.

May he give you your heart's desire,
the fulfilment of all you plan;
we will shout for joy, we will sing,
and celebrate the name of our God.

Now I know that the Lord
gives victory to the King of his choice;
he speaks from his holy height
with saving deeds of power.

Chariots and horses their strength,
but our trust is the name of God;
they will stumble and fall,
while we stand upright and firm.

Lord, give victory to the King,
answer us whenever we call.

Psalm 20 *(Heb. 21)*

Antiphon: We will praise you, Lord, for your might,
we will sing and proclaim your power.

The King rejoices, O Lord, in your strength,
he is glad because of the victory you gave;
from you he has received his heart's desire,
you did not refuse the request of his lips.

You poured out blessings beyond compare,
on his head you set a diadem of gold;
he asked for life, you gave him his desire:
a long, a lasting life you bestowed.

Great is his glory, for you are his help,
you have put upon him majesty and fame;
Yes, for ever your blessings will endure,
you have crowned him with joy before your face.

Yes, the King puts his trust in the Lord,
the love of the Almighty will keep him secure;
his hand will come down on all his foes,
his right hand will seize them and hold them fast.

We will praise you, Lord, for your might,
we will sing and proclaim your power.

Psalm 21 *(Heb. 22)*

Antiphon: We worship you, Lord, upon the Cross,
and your Resurrection in power we proclaim.

My God, my God, why have you abandoned me?
Far from my cry, from the sound of my prayer!
By day I call, you make no reply,
when I call in the night, no respite comes.

Yet you are enthroned on high,
Holy God of Israel's praise;
in you our fathers put their faith,
they trusted you and they were saved;
when they cried to you, they escaped,
their hope was never in vain.

But I am no man, a mere worm,
scorned and mocked by all in the streets;
if any behold me, they laugh,
they scoff, then they shake their heads:
'He trusts in God! Let him save him,
deliver him, if truly he cares!'

It was you that took me at birth,
you loved me in my mother's arms;
since the day I was born, you have held me,
from the womb, you have been my God;
do not go away, the agony is near,
and see, I have no help.

Like wild beasts they gather around,
fierce bulls to left and to right,
their jaws are flashing wide
like lions devouring their prey.

Like water, my strength is dried up,
my bones are all out of joint;
my heart is like melted wax,
dissolving within my breast;
my throat is dry like dust,
my tongue cleaves to the roof of my mouth.

The wolves crowd around me in wait,
evil men closing in for the kill;
they have pierced my hands and my feet;
I am left for dead in the dust.

I can number all my bones,
my enemies stand now and stare;
they begin to share out my clothes,
for my garments they are casting lots.

Do not stay far away, O Lord,
my strength, come quickly, save me;
rescue my soul from the sword,
my life from the prowling dogs;
deliver my soul from the beasts,
save me from the horns of the bull.

I will proclaim to my brethren your name,
where the people gather for praise;
bless the Lord, all who serve him,
sons of Jacob, honour his name,
worship him, Israel's sons.

He neither neglects nor ignores
the afflictions that befall the poor,
he does not veil his face,
when they cry, he hears their prayer.

To you I give thanks in the Assembly of praise,
performing my vows before all who love God;
the poor shall eat until they are filled,
all who come to the Lord will give him praise:
may they flourish and prosper, year after year.

The farthest ends of the earth will see and recall,
every nation will turn and bow down to the Lord;
the Kingdom is God's, he is Master of the world;
the children of men will draw near and adore,
all mortal flesh will fall to worship his name.

And my race shall live for him, my children serve,
proclaiming the Lord to ages unborn,
his justice to nations yet to come:
    Such are God's deeds!

Psalm 22 *(Heb. 23)*

Antiphon: My Shepherd is the Lord,
see, how my cup overflows!

——

The Lord is my shepherd,
so nothing I shall lack;
he leads me across green fields,
and there I find rest;
he brings me to quiet waters
where he quenches my thirst.

He guides me along safe paths,
because of his love.
When the hills loom dark around
I shall fear no harm,
you are close with your rod and staff,
to deliver my soul.

You spread before me a banquet
when the enemy draws near;
you perfume my head with oil,
my cup overflows.

Your goodness and kindness will pursue
every day of my life;
in the house of the Lord I will live
through the ages to come.

Psalm 23 *(Heb. 24)*

Antiphon: Open wide, gates of everlasting praise,
rise up and hail the King of Glory.

All the earth, and its fullness, is the Lord's,
the world, with all that it contains;
he founded and built it in the deep,
grounded it firm in the flood.

Who may ascend the Mountain of the Lord,
who may enter his Holy Place?
One with clean hands, a pure heart,
who is not set on falsehood and wrong.

On him is the blessing of the Lord,
the favour of his saving God;
for such is the race of those who seek,
who long for your face, O Lord.

Gates, lift up your heads,
open wide, eternal doors,
here is the King of Glory!

Who is the King of Glory?
It is God, almighty and strong,
our God, victorious in war.

Gates, lift up your heads,
open wide, eternal doors,
here is the King of Glory!

Who is the King of Glory?
It is God, Lord of all the worlds,
he is the King of Glory!

Psalm 24 *(Heb. 25)*

Antiphon: To you, O Lord, I lift up my soul in hope,
for when we trust in you, we are not deceived.

To you, O Lord, I lift up my soul,
to you, my God.

In you I trust, let me not be put to shame,
let my foes have no cause to exult;
I have faith, I shall not be put to shame,
but woe to all who rebel.

Teach me, Lord, and show me your ways,
O God, let me learn your paths,
instruct me in the truth of your Law,
for you are my Saviour and my God.

In you, all day long, I hope
because of your compassion, O Lord;
remember your kindness, O God,
and your goodness, as ever of old;
forgive all the errors of my youth
and remember me, Lord, in your love.

The Lord is righteous and good,
he leads sinners back to his ways,
he guides the humble in justice,
to the simple he reveals his will.

All his paths are faithfulness and love,
to all who keep his commands.
According to your promises, O God,
forgive all my many sins.

Is there one that would honour the Lord?
He will guide him in the path he must choose;
all his days will be days of joy,
his children will possess the land;
the Lord is close to all who obey him,
he gives them his covenant and truth.

I lift up my eyes to the Lord,
for he frees my feet from the snare;
see how weak and lonely I am,
come soon, have mercy on me.

Relieve the torments of my heart,
console my soul in distress;
see my anguish and my pain,
forgive me for all my sins.

See how many are my foes,
with what hatred I am despised;
save me, deliver my soul,
give me shelter, keep me from shame;
may goodness and justice be my guards,
in you I trust, O God.

Psalm 25 *(Heb. 26)*

Antiphon: Lord how I love all the beauty of your house,
the place of your glory, O God!

——

Give sentence for me, O Lord!
See, I do what is right,
I believe in God, with all my heart.

Test me now and fathom my thoughts,
discern all the longing of my heart;
your constant love is my guide,
I will walk in the steps of your truth.

I will not sit with those who love wrong,
with the hypocrites I do not consort,
I hate their gatherings of evil,
from the wicked I turn my steps aside.

In Innocence I wash my hands,
I worship at your altar, O Lord;
my tongue sings out hymns of praise,
I will tell all the wonders you have done.

Do not count me as one who does wrong,
see, my hands are not stained with blood;
though many do evil all day long,
their hands ever open for bribes.

As for me, I do what is right,
Lord, redeem me, have mercy on me;
my foot stands firm, I am safe,
I will praise you with your people, O Lord.

Psalm 26 *(Heb. 27)*

Antiphon: The Lord shall be my light and my defence;
his house shall be my dwelling.

The Lord is my light and my salvation,
so whom should I fear?
The Lord keeps my soul from harm,
then why be afraid?

When the men of evil ways draw near,
to destroy my life,
it is they, my rivals and my foes,
who stumble and fall.

Though an army lies camped around,
my heart will not fear;
though war be declared on my soul,
I will not lose hope.

One thing that I ask of the Lord,
the thing that I seek:
to dwell in the house of the Lord
all the days of my life,
to marvel at the goodness of God
and to pray for help.

I will shelter beneath his tent
when troubles arise
and there, in his Temple, I hide,
in safety on the rock.

In triumph, he lifts up my head,
high above all my foes;
in his tent I will sacrifice with praise
glad offerings of joy.

Pay heed, O Lord, when I call,
have mercy, reply!
My heart repeats your words:
seek his face.

O Lord, I am seeking your face,
do not hide your face;
do not cast away your servant in wrath,
you were always my help.

No, do not forsake me, O Lord,
my Saviour, my God;
if my father and mother deny me,
with you I shall find love.

So guide me along safe paths
and teach me your ways;
bitter foes attack me with lies,
do not leave me, O God.

I shall see God's goodness, I know,
in this present life;
take heart, trust in God and believe,
put your hope in the Lord.

Psalm 29 *(Heb. 30)*

Antiphon: I will praise you Lord, for you have raised me up,
never you allow my enemies to triumph.

I cried out to you for help,
by you, O God, I was healed.
O Lord, you have snatched my life from the grave,
you restored me to life, though I stood at death's door.

Rejoice in the Lord, all his saints,
give thanks for his holy deeds.
For a moment his anger, a lifetime his love,
night falls with weeping, but day breaks in song.

Boasting in prosperity I said:
Nothing can ever bring me down.
In your favour I stood as firm as the hills,
then you hid your face and I was afraid.

To you, O Lord, I called out,
I implored your mercy, O God.
What good is my blood, will you gain by my death?
Will the dust give you praise or proclaim your truth?

Have mercy, hear me, O Lord,
O God, come to my aid!
You took my sorrow to make it a dance,
you stripped off my grief and clothed me with joy.

So my heart will not cease to sing your praise,
O Lord my God, I will ever give you thanks.

Psalm 30 *(Heb. 31)*

I

Antiphon: Into your hands I commend my spirit,
for you have saved me, O Lord.

I take shelter in you, O Lord,
I shall never be put to shame;
you are just, make haste to save me,
incline your ear to my prayer.

Be for me a rock of defence,
a fortress to keep me safe;
Lord, you are my fortress and rock,
so guide me, for your promise is sure.

Keep me safe from the traps they have laid,
for in you I trust;
into your hands I commend my spirit,
for you have saved me, O Lord.

God of truth, you detest
all those who serve false gods;
but I will rejoice and be glad
on account of your constant love.

Lord, you saw my distress,
you beheld the trouble of my soul;
you saved me from my enemies' hands,
your love led me out, set me free.

Have pity on me, O Lord,
for distress is upon me;
my eyes are consumed with tears,
my body and my soul.

For see, I am weary with grief,
    my life has wasted in tears;
my strength has faded away
    and my bones are destroyed.

My enemies treat me with contempt,
    all my neighbours mock;
my friends shudder at my sight,
    in the streets they flee.

I am banished from living mind,
    as though I were dead,
rejected and thrown aside
    like a thing of no use.

II

Antiphon: Blessed be the Lord, my defence,
he shows wonders of love.

——

I hear the muttering of crowds,
    fear on every side!
They are plotting together against me
    to take away my life.

But always I trust in you, O Lord,
    you see, you are my God;
all my life lies in your hand,
    save me from the hands of my foes.

Look kindly on your servant, O Lord,
    save me by your love;
let me not be ashamed when I pray,
    shame on wicked-doers.

Let silence and night be their lot,
their lies fall still,
the insolent who insult the just,
so arrogant and proud.

How wonderful is your goodness, O Lord,
the goodness you show your friends;
you are good for all who believe,
in the eyes of all mankind.

In your presence, you keep them hid,
safe from intrigues of men;
you conceal them all in your tent,
far from the cursing of tongues.

Yet once I thought in my grief:
'He has lost me from sight.'
but I called out and you heard my cry
as I pleaded for help.

So love the Lord, all his saints!
He takes care of all his friends;
but he claims a high price indeed
from all who are proud.

The Lord, my defence, he bless'd,
he shows wonders of love;
be brave and be of good heart,
all who hope in the Lord.

Psalm 31 *(Heb. 32)*

Antiphon: I said: I will go to my father,
and confess my fault.

Happy men, absolved of your sins,
and whose faults are forgiven;
happy souls, to whom our Lord
will impute no blame
and whose hearts are clear.

I would not speak, and my bones were consumed,
all the day I wept;
by day and by night your hand
bore down on my soul;
my strength was dried up like the dew
in the midday sun.

At last, I confessed all my guilt,
no longer I denied my shame,
I said, 'I will go to the Lord
and confess my fault!'
Then you absolved my sin,
you forgave every wrong.

So now your people should pray
in their times of need;
when the waters flow high in flood,
they are not overwhelmed;
you give me refuge and peace,
I am safe from harm. (. . .)

Psalm 32 *(Heb. 33)*

Antiphon: Cry out for joy to God our Lord, all his saints;
praise is good when the heart is true!

Cry out for joy to the Lord, all his saints,
praise is good when the heart is true.

Offer thanks to the Lord with the harp,
praise God to the sound of the lyre;
sign out new songs to the Lord,
on the harp play hymns to his praise.

True are the words of the Lord,
most faithful are all his works;
he delights in justice and right,
the earth overflows with his love.

By his command, the heavens came to be,
all the stars by the words of his mouth;
he gathered the sea in one place
and enclosed the deep in his store.

All the earth, worship the Lord,
let every nation adore;
he spoke, and the world was made,
he commanded and all stood fast.

He undoes all the nations' designs,
he frustrates all of their plans;
the designs of the Lord endure,
everlasting, the plan of his heart.

Happy land, whose God is the Lord,
the people he has chosen as his own;
from on high, the Lord looks down
and beholds all the children of men.

From the height of his glory he observes
all who dwell on the earth;
he fashions their every thought,
he knows all that they do.

No army can give triumph to a king;
no strength can keep a swordsman safe;
what man gained victory by a horse?
No hope, for all its speed.

But the Lord has eyes for his friends,
all whose trust is set in his love;
he will keep their souls from death,
sustain them in times of need.

Let our hope be set in the Lord,
for he is our help and our shield;
in God, the joy of our hearts,
our trust, his holy name!

On us, O Lord, be your love,
as we place our hope in you.
Praise Father, Son and Holy Spirit,
for ever and ever. Amen.

Psalm 33 *(Heb. 34)*

Antiphon: Yes, I will bless the Lord at all times,
on my lips the sound of his praises.

I will bless the Lord at all times,
on my lips, the sound of his praise;
give glory, my soul, to the Lord,
all the humble, hear and rejoice.

Come, let us worship the Lord,
with one voice give glory to God;
I cried to the Lord, he replied,
he freed me when I was afraid.

With God is the fullness of joys,
turn to him, you will not be deceived;
when the poor cry out, he gives heed,
he is close to all in distress.

The angel of God is near,
he defends the faithful of heart;
how good is the Lord! Taste and see!
What joy when he is our guard!

Adore the Lord, all his saints,
he takes care of his friends in need;
the lions may go hungry, in want,
but the godly will lack nothing good.

Now come, children, pay heed,
I will teach you the service of the Lord;
is there one who longs for life,
to delight in the blessings of days?

Keep your tongue from all that may hurt,
let your lips not utter deceit;
refrain from wrong and do good,
strive for peace with all your heart.

The eyes of the Lord are on the just,
his ears are open to their prayer;
while all who do evil are destroyed,
their names erased from the earth.

In anguish, the just call on God,
he saves them from all their distress;
broken hearts are dear to the Lord,
he raises their souls from despair.

On the just, evils rain down,
but the Lord will save them from all;
he will guard them with tender care,
not one of their bones will be bruised.

But evil destroys the unjust,
those who hate the godly will die;
the Lord has mercy on his friends,
no one turns to our God in vain.

Psalm 34 (extract) *(Heb. 35)*

Antiphon: Of your goodness my tongue will sing,
all day long, O Lord, your praise.

Accuse, Lord, for I am accused,
attack them—I am attacked;
take up your armour and your shield,
stand up, be my help.

Brandish both sword and lance
in the face of those who pursue;
O Lord, speak thus to my soul:
It is I, I will save.

Then my soul will rejoice in the Lord,
exult, for I am saved;
all my bones will cry out: O Lord,
who then is like you,
saving the weak from the hands of the strong,
the poor that they all exploit?

Their witnesses stand up, telling lies,
what they ask I do not know;
they repay me with evil for good,
my soul becomes dry.

They were sick, then sackcloth I wore,
in fasting I bowed
and murmured prayers in my heart,
as if for a brother or friend,
I wept as if my mother had died,
overwhelmed in my grief.

How much longer, O Lord, will you look?
    Draw my soul from their hands,
    from the lions save my life!
In the Assembly then I will give thanks,
in the multitude I will give praise.

Break silence, O Master, you have seen,
    do not stay far away;
awake, stand up in my defence,
    give me justice, Lord my God.

Then all will laugh, shout for joy,
    rejoicing that I am found just;
constantly I hear them exclaim:
    Great is our God,
for he wills that his servant see peace!

Of your goodness my tongue will sing,
    all day long, O Lord, your praise!

Psalm 35 *(Heb. 36)*

Antiphon: In you, O Lord, is the source of life,
by your light we see true light.

The wisdom of the wicked is sin
deep in his heart;
no sign of respect for God
in all that he does.

He esteems himself too much,
'My sin is not known!'
All his words are lies and deceit,
he does nothing good.

Instead of good, he plans wrong,
even while he sleeps;
he persists in ways that are not good,
refusing to repent.

O Lord, in the heavens, your love!
Your truth, with the clouds!
Your justice, high as the hills!
Your goodness, like the sea!

You care for both man and beast,
O God, how precious is your love;
the people you defend, O Lord,
find shelter in the shadow of your wings.

We are filled at the feasts in your courts,
refreshed by your living streams;
in you is the source of life,
by your light, we see true light.

Stay close to your friends, O Lord,
be good for all who are just;
save us from the malice of the proud
that their hands do not drive us away.

Psalm 37 *(Heb. 38)*

Antiphon: Do not forsake me, my Lord,
do not stay away, O God.

O Lord, do not punish me in rage,
in wrath, do not chastise me, my God.

Your arrows have wounded my flesh,
your hand has struck me to the ground;
through your anger, nothing but pain,
for my sins, my body lies sick.

My sins are a flood where I drown,
a burden too heavy to bear;
bowed down and bent with shame,
I go mourning all day long.

With fever my flesh is on fire,
my body is sick to death;
worn out and numb with pain,
I groan in the anguish of my heart.

You know all my longing, O Lord,
you can hear my every sigh;
how my heart pounds in my breast,
my sight and my strength grow faint.

My friends and neighbours draw back,
they stare at my sores from afar;
what snares men have laid for my life,
those who are plotting to kill.

I am deaf, for all that I hear,
like the dumb, my lips are sealed;
it seems that I cannot hear,
for to no one I make reply.

But in you, O Lord, is my trust,
and you are the one who will speak;
they shall not rejoice at my pain,
nor must they laugh at my fall.

See, I am almost dead,
my torment is always at hand;
yes, I admit my guilt,
I shudder for all my sins.

My foes are so healthy and strong,
they are many that hate me for no cause;
they repay all my kindness with harm,
they blame me for what I did right.

So do not forsake me, my Lord,
do not stay away, O God;
quickly, come to my aid,
Lord, my Saviour, my God.

Psalm 38 *(Heb. 39)*

Antiphon: Lord, to whom shall we go?
You have the words of eternal life.

I said, 'I must always take care,
I will watch what I say and not sin,
I will curb my tongue and not speak
while the wicked are standing near.'
So I stood there, silent and still,
but my torment only grew worse.

My heart was on fire in my breast,
from my thoughts sprang up tongues of flame;
so at last I ventured to speak:
'O Lord, let me know my end;
what is the span of my days?
Remind me how little is a life.

How small is the number of my days,
before you my life is naught;
our human span is one breath,
then we pass away like a shade;
our deeds are one breath of wind.
Our riches? A stranger's joy.'

So what can I hope for, O Lord?
I will wait, I will rest in you;
only save me from sin,
and save me from the mockery of fools;
I am quiet, I will not say one word,
since you are the Author of all.

But spare our backs from the scourge,
strike us no more—we shall die;
with rebukes, you chasten our guilt,
while all that we love dissolves
like a moth, like a breath of air;
receive my prayer, O God.

Pay heed to my heart's request,
do not ignore all my tears;
I am only a pilgrim on earth,
your guest, as my fathers were;
turn aside for a while, let me breathe,
before I must rise and be gone.

Psalm 39 *(Heb. 40)*

Antiphon: All who long for your face shall be glad,
rejoicing and songs!

——

I hoped in the Lord with firm hope,
he heard the sound of my voice,
he paid heed to my cry.

He pulled me out of the pit,
from the quicksand's snare;
he set my feet on the rock
and I stood secure.

In my mouth he put a new song:
praise to our God!
Many shall see and shall fear,
they will trust in the Lord.

How happy, the people who believe,
who have faith in the Lord,
not taking the way of the proud
who run to false gods.

Such great works you have done, O Lord!
Vast wonders untold!
All manner of plans for our good,
too many they are to count!

No sacrifice, no offering you ask,
but our ears for your word;
burnt-sacrifice you do not require:
I said, 'Here I am.'

In the book, my part is laid down:
    your will, O God;
how I long to do your will,
    your Law is stamped on my heart.

My lips have proclaimed your good news
    to the people around;
Yes, I spoke, I did not refrain,
    you saw and you know.

Your love does not stay concealed
    in my silent heart;
all the time, I proclaim your truth,
    to the people, your grace.

Your mercy is vast, without end,
    for me, O Lord;
preserve me by your kindness and truth
    all the days of my life.

But evils come crowding around,
    more than the hairs on my head;
on my back my sins rain down,
    my heart grows faint.

Save me, O Lord, be my help!
    Rescue me, my God!
Let those who would destroy my life
    all be put to shame.

Those who look and rejoice at my distress
    shall retreat in disgrace;
and the people who enjoy my grief
    —let them say: we were fools.

All who long for your face shall be glad,
rejoicing and songs!
Let those who enjoy your peace
say: How great is our God!

Your servant is weak and so poor,
but you do not forget;
Yes, you are my Saviour and my God,
make haste to my aid.

Psalm 40 *(Heb. 41)*

Antiphon: Your hand will guide me, I will stand,
alive you will set me before your face.

How happy all who care for the poor,
on the day of distress, the Lord is their help;
the Lord is their guard, their Saviour and joy,
never shall they fall into the power of their foes;
the Lord is there, whenever they fall sick,
he restores their health if their strength grows weak.

I said in my heart: Take pity on me, Lord!
Heal my soul for against you I have sinned.
All my enemies laugh as they wait for me to die:
When will he die and his name be destroyed?
At my bedside they talk, but their words ring false
—their malice is hid, they gossip outside.

As my foes embrace they exchange bad news,
for them my distress is a source of delight:
His body is wracked with a dreadful disease,
it is sure he will not rise again from his bed!
Even my companion, the friend I love most,
who once was my guest now stands with my foes.

O Lord, be merciful, restore me to health,
let them see your power, they shall be repaid;
they will all be disgraced, since you are my friend
—your hand will guide me, I will stand,
alive, you will set me before your face!
Give praise to our God for ever, Amen!

Psalm 41 *(Heb. 42)*

Antiphon: My soul is thirsting for the Lord,
when shall I see him face to face?

Like a deer that yearns
for a cooling stream,
so my soul is athirst
for you, my God.

My soul is thirsting for God,
for the living God;
when shall I come and behold
the face of God?

Tears are my only food
by night and by day;
always I hear them say:
Where is your God?

Once I went with the throng
to the House of our God,
with shouts of rejoicing and praise
on the lips of the crowd.

What weighs you down, my soul?
Why faint in my breast?
Hope in God: I will praise him still,
my Saviour, my God.

When my heart is about to break
I turn my thoughts
from Jordan and Hermon's land,
from the lowly hill.

The deep summoning the deep,
    the roaring of the flood!
The might of your raging waves
    overwhelms my soul.

If by day the Lord is pleased
    to reveal his love,
his song in my heart by night
    prays the God of my life.

I implore my defender, my God:
    Why did you forget?
Why must I now go in grief,
    oppressed by the foe?

All my bones are crushed with shame
    at the insults I endure;
always I hear them say:
    Where is your God?

What weighs you down, my soul?
    Why faint in my breast?
Hope in God: I will praise him still,
    my Saviour, my God.

Psalm 42 *(Heb. 43)*

Antiphon: I will go to the altar of God,
he is the fountain of joy!

Give sentence in my favour, O God,
against the godless men;
from the power of the wicked and the false
deliver my soul.

For you are my defender, O God,
why cast me aside?
And why must I endure such pain
at the hands of my foes?

Send out your light and your truth,
let them be my guides;
bring me back to your holy hill,
to the house where you dwell.

I will go to the altar of God,
he is the fountain of joy;
I will play on the harp, I will sing
to praise you, O God.

What weighs you down, my soul?
Why faint in my breast?
Hope in God: I will praise him still,
my Saviour, my God.

Psalm 44 (extract) *(Heb. 45)*

Antiphon: For ever, O God, you throne on high,
justice, your sceptre, for the people you rule.

My heart overflows with beautiful words,
hear the song I have made for the king,
my tongue is dancing to nimble words!

You are far more handsome than all other men,
such graceful eloquence flows from your lips,
surely you are blessed in the eyes of God.

Gird now your sword, great king, at your side,
ride on in might, most glorious lord,
for truth and justice pursue your way.

Perform great deeds, for your arrows are sharp,
the peoples lie still, nations fall at your feet;
to see your power, your enemies lose heart.

For ever, O God, you throne on high,
justice, your sceptre, for the people you rule,
you are just of heart, injustice you abhor.

So God, who chose you, anoints your head,
with perfumes of gladness he marks your brow,
your robes are fragrant with aloes and myrrh. (. . .)

Psalm 45 *(Heb. 46)*

Antiphon: Our help is the Lord of hosts,
no fortress other than Jacob's God.

God is with us, our shelter and strength,
our help in distress, he is close at hand;
then how should we fear, though the earth gives way
or the mountains are hurled to the depths of the sea?
If waves come pounding with violence and rage,
so that hills are shaken by the breakers' roar.

Our help is the Lord of hosts,
no fortress other than Jacob's God.

Like a stream, joy flows to the house of God,
its waters gladden his holy place;
God is there, it cannot be destroyed,
God will send help at the dawn of day;
the nations tremble, great kingdoms shake,
he lifts up his voice, the earth melts away.

Our help is the Lord of hosts,
no fortress other than Jacob's God.

Behold and see what the Lord has done,
deeds that fill the whole world with awe;
his hand stops wars to the ends of the earth,
bows he has broken, lances destroyed,
'Now be still, and confess that I am God,
supreme in all nations, supreme upon earth!'

Our help is the Lord of hosts,
no fortress other than Jacob's God.

Psalm 46 *(Heb. 47)*

Antiphon: Clap your hands for joy, all the world,
sing out to God, to his holy name.

Clap your hands for joy, all the world,
sing out to God, to his holy name;
for the Lord, the Most High is to be feared,
great King to the ends of the earth.

He brings the nations to our feet,
great peoples under our yoke;
he has chosen a land where we may live,
the pride of the people he loves.

God goes up in shouts of joy,
the Lord, to the trumpet-blast;
sing praises to God, sing praise;
praise to our King, sing praise.

He is King over all the world,
so praise him with music and song;
he rules the nations of the earth,
set high on his sacred throne.

The rulers of the world unite
with the people of Abraham's God;
all the might of the earth is the Lord's,
on high he reigns supreme.

Psalm 47 *(Heb. 48)*

Antiphon: We remember your love,
in your courts, O Lord.

Great is the Lord and worthy of all praise
in the city of our God!
His holy hill is the fairest of all,
joy for all the world.

Here is Zion, the mountain of God,
and the city of kings;
God, for all in her walls,
is a sure defence.

Great kings took council for war,
they advanced to attack;
when they saw, they were struck with dread,
full of awe, they took flight.

There, they trembled with fear,
like a woman in birth,
great ships broken on the rocks
by the fury of the storm.

As we had heard, now we have seen
how great is the Lord;
in the city of the Lord of hosts:
he is forever our strength.

We remember your love, O God,
in the courts of the Lord;
your fame and your praise, O God,
have covered the earth.

You govern the nations with right,
    let Zion be glad;
let the cities of Judah rejoice
    for your judgements are good.

Come to Zion, examine with care
    the number of her towers,
inspect her fortresses with awe,
    take note of her walls.

You shall tell your children in turn:
    This God is our God;
for all time, for evermore,
    he is our guide.

Psalm 50 *(Heb. 51)*

Antiphon: Have mercy on me, God, in your love,
I confess the wrongs I have done,
you will give me again songs of gladness.

Have mercy on me, God in your love,
in your compassion blot out all my sin;
wash away the stain of my faults,
let me be pure from all my misdeeds.

I will confess the wrong I have done,
I remember all my sins;
I have sinned against you alone,
I have done what is evil in your sight.

So now it is right that I be judged,
with reason I am condemned;
yes, in sin I was born,
at fault from my mother's womb.

You require sincerity of heart,
so instruct me in the depths of your truth;
wipe out my sins, that I may be clean,
and wash me whiter than snow.

Give me the sound of gladness and joy,
let the bones you have broken dance;
turn your face from all my faults,
wipe out all trace of my sins.

So give me, O God, a pure heart,
my spirit make new within;
do not thrust me far from your face,
do not take your Spirit away.

Give me back the joy of your love,
a heart willing to obey;
I will teach transgressors your ways,
the lost will return to your path.

Save me from guilt, O God, and from death,
your justice shall become my song;
O Lord, open my lips
and my mouth shall proclaim your praise.

You desire no sacrifice, O Lord,
burnt offerings you would not accept;
all I offer is a contrite heart,
a broken heart you will not disdain.

Be kind to Zion, for her joy,
build high Jerusalem's walls;
you will accept the sacrifice we bring,
all we offer at the foot of your throne.

Psalm 53 *(Heb. 54)*

Antiphon: God will come to my aid,
the Lord will sustain my life.

O God, save me in your might,
by your power, deliver my soul;
O Lord, give heed to my prayer,
and hear the words of my mouth.

Against me have risen proud men,
fierce and cruel, they are after my blood,
but God will come to my aid,
the Lord will sustain my life.

I will worship you in gladness of heart,
O God, I will praise your name;
you are good, you saved me in distress,
you have put my enemies to flight.

Psalm 54 *(Heb. 55)*

Antiphon: Confide all your burdens to the Lord,
he will be your defence.

Give ear to my prayer, O God,
do not turn from my cry;
listen, and answer me soon,
I am worn out with cares.

I tremble at the threats of my foes,
the wicked beat me down;
they bring trouble raining on my head,
their hatred knows no bounds.

So my heart is stricken with fear,
almost crushed to death;
with fear and trembling I was seized,
overwhelmed with dread.

If I only had wings like a dove,
to fly away and rest,
I would flee to a distant land,
to a desert waste.

I long to find refuge soon
from the raging storm;
let them all be scattered, O Lord,
in confusion of tongues.

For violence roams the town,
I see strife on every side;
by day and by night they prowl
high on the walls.

Within flourish crime and wrong,
    while destruction thrives,
oppression parades through the streets,
    fraud hides at every turn.

If the insults had come from a foe,
    that, I could bear;
if my rivals persist in their threats,
    then I can hide.

But you, my companion, my friend,
    the brother of my heart!
How often we talked in times past
    as we went up to pray.

I lift up my voice to God,
    I am sure he will come;
by morning, at noon and at night,
    my groans rise up.

The Lord will save me in peace
    from the warfare I face;
so many are rising against me,
    but he hears my prayer . . .

Confide all your burdens to the Lord,
    he will be your defence;
he will not permit the just
    to suffer defeat.

Psalm 55 *(Heb. 56)*

Antiphon: I will give you worship and praise,
for you have rescued my soul from death.

Have mercy, my enemies attack,
they persecute me all the day long;
at all hours my opponents attack,
against me so many lie in wait.

Most High, at times when I fear,
in you I place my trust;
I praise God because of his Word,
I trust and am no longer afraid;
what can they do to me now?

All day they seek to do me harm,
to hurt me, the sole aim of their plans;
they gather, they hide, keeping watch,
lying in wait for my life.

You take note of the troubles I endure,
and your flask is full of my tears;
all the day I invoke your name,
so my enemies will be turned aside.

I know that God is on my side,
I praise him because of his Word,
God be praised for all his words!
I will trust him and no longer be afraid:
what more can they do to me now?

O God, I am bound by my vows,
I will give you worship and praise;
for you have rescued my soul from death,
so I will walk in the presence of God,
in the light of all who live.

Psalm 56 *(Heb. 57)*

Antiphon: Show your greatness. O God, in the heavens,
your glory on the earth.

Have mercy on me, God, have mercy,
I seek refuge in you for my soul;
I find shelter in the shadow of your wings,
until the storms have passed.

I call to God, the Most High,
to God who takes care of every need;
he will send down from heaven and save me,
he will put my oppressors to flight;

I am cast among roaring lions,
they devour the children of men:
their teeth are like arrows and spears,
their tongues are like sharp-edged swords.

Show your greatness, O God, in the heavens,
    your glory on the earth!
They spread out a net for my feet,
    my soul was overwhelmed;
in my path they dug out a pit,
    but fell into it themselves!

My heart is fixed, O God,
    my heart is fixed;
I will sing, I will give praise to your name:
    awake now, my soul!
Awake now, lute and harp,
    I will arouse the dawn.

Among the nations, I will give praise,
    give thanks in every land;
high as the heavens is your love,
    your truth as the clouds;
reveal your greatness in the heavens,
    your glory on the earth.

Psalm 60 *(Heb. 61)*

Antiphon: Without end, I will praise your name,
fulfilling my vows, day by day.

Hear my cry, O God,
give heed to my prayer;
from the ends of the earth I call,
my heart grows faint.

O God, set me high on the rock,
and give me your rest;
for you are my refuge, O Lord,
beside you I am safe.

May I always live in your Tent;
and keep me beneath your wings!
For you have heard my vows, O God,
you bless me like all who love your name.

Add long days to the life of the King,
generation on generation, his years!
May he reign for ever in your presence, O God,
may his guards be always your Kindness and Truth.

Without end, I will praise your name,
fulfilling my vows, day by day.

Psalm 61 *(Heb. 62)*

Antiphon: In God I find glory and peace,
my defender is God!

With God I find rest for my soul,
salvation he brings;
for he is my Saviour, my Rock,
my stronghold of defence.

How long will you fall on a man,
and batter him down,
like any crumbling wall
or a broken-down fence?

Their only desire is to destroy,
and lies are their delight;
with their lips they sweetly bless,
while in their hearts they curse.

With God take your rest, my soul,
for in him is my hope;
he alone is my Saviour, my Rock,
my stronghold of defence;
in God I find glory and peace,
my defender is God.

At all times have trust in him,
my people, hear!
Pour out before him your hearts,
our defender is God.

Mankind is only a breath,
great and small alike;
if all of them mount on the scales,
they are less than the wind.

Do not put any trust in force,
    crime brings no reward;
on wealth, if riches abound,
    do not set your heart.

One word I heard God speak,
    these two I have heard:
that all power belongs to our God,
    he is constant in love;
and that you will reward us all
    as our deeds deserve.

Psalm 62 *(Heb. 63)*

Antiphon: O God, my God,
my body is pining for your presence,
I seek your face at dawn.

God, you are my God, I seek your face at dawn,
my soul is thirsting for you,
my body is pining for you,
parched ground, waterless and dry;
in the Sanctuary, I long to adore you,
to behold your glory and power.

Your love is better than life,
my lips will proclaim your praise;
all my life, I would bless you,
my hands lifted up in prayer;
my soul feasting till satisfied,
joy on my lips, praise in my mouth.

When I think of you, as I sleep,
remember you all through the night;
you have been my help,
I rejoice in the shadow of your wings;
my soul finds rest at your side,
your right hand is holding me safe.

Psalm 64 *(Heb. 65)*

Antiphon: God will come to the earth
and he will bless it;
he will bless our meadows,
all the fields will shout for joy.

It is good to praise you, O God,
to praise you in Zion;
to you all vows shall be performed,
for you answer our prayer.

To you all flesh shall come,
on account of our sins;
our guilt is greater than our strength,
but you will forgive.

Happy are they whom you choose,
and bring to your courts;
we shall all be filled with your gifts,
the blessings of your House.

Your justice is wonderful for us,
you save us, O God!
The Hope of the ends of the earth
and the distant seas.

The mountains arose by your might,
to manifest your power;
your hand silences the sea,
the raging of its waves.

All the nations in tumult fall still,
their peoples stand in awe;
from sunrise to sunset you are hailed
with wonder and joy.

You come to give rain to the fields,
    to make their soil rich;
the streams run full to the brim,
    you take care of our needs.

On the fields you send abundant rain,
    the furrows drink their fill;
by your showers, the soil becomes soft,
    and you bless the seed.

Your goodness sets a crown on the year,
the harvests overflow as you pass,
the fields of the desert give their fruit.

The hills, radiant with delight,
the pastures, adorned with flocks of sheep,
the valleys resplendent with wheat:
all laugh, all shout for joy!

Psalm 65 *(Heb. 66)*

Antiphon: All the earth, O God,
comes in awe before your throne,
singing songs of praise,
singing for your Name.

Sing praise to God, all the earth,
and sing to the glory of his Name;
give praise with glorious praise,
say to God: How great are your deeds!

Your deeds are as great as your power,
your enemies bow down in fear;
all the earth adores you with awe,
singing praise, the praise of your Name.

Come, see the works of our God,
what wonders he has done among men:
he changed the sea into firm ground,
we crossed the river dry-shod.

So let our joy be in him,
our God of unending might;
he watches the nations, alert,
no rebel can aspire to his throne.

Let the peoples bless our God,
and sing to the Lord with praise;
for he restored us to life,
he kept us safe from the fall.

We were put to the test, O God,
you tried us like silver, with fire;
you let us fall into a trap,
you laid great burdens on our backs.

The foe tramped over our heads,
we went through fire and flood;
but now you have made us safe.

In your Courts I will sacrifice with praise,
as I promised, now I will perform:
the vows that I made with my mouth,
my words in the days of distress.

Draw near, all who honour our God,
I will tell you great things he has done:
I spoke, I called on his Name,
my lips always full of his praise;

if sin had been found in my heart,
he would not have granted my prayer;
but God gave heed to my voice,
he answered me when I called.

All praise to God!
He did not reject my prayer,
he never withholds his love.

Psalm 66 *(Heb. 67)*

Antiphon: To you, God, are the praises of nations,
all the nations give you glory and praise, O God.

O God, show your mercy and bless us,
and look upon us with love;
all the earth will know your ways,
all the nations your power to save.

To you, God, are the praises of nations,
all the nations give you glory and praise, O God!

Let the nations rejoice and be glad,
for great is your justice for the world;
you judge the peoples with right,
and guide all the nations of the earth.

To you, God, are the praises of nations,
all the nations give you glory and praise, O God!

The earth has yielded its fruit,
God, our God has bless'd us;
may God be bless'd and adored,
to all the ends of the earth.

To you, God, are the praises of nations,
all the nations give you glory and praise, O God!

Psalm 67 *(Heb. 68)*

Antiphon: Our mighty Salvation delivers us from all,
our God is Lord of the gateways of death.

Let God arise, and his enemies are put to flight,
all his rivals are scattered in defeat;
as smoke blows away, so they are dispersed,
like wax that melts in front of the fire,
so are the wicked before the face of God.

But the just exult to behold God's face,
they all rejoice, they dance for joy;
sing to God, sing praises to his name,
make way for the one who rides on the clouds,
his name is the Lord, be glad before his face.

Father of orphans, the widows' defence,
such is God in his Holy Place;
he gives the forsaken a home where they can live,
he opens for prisoners the gateway to bliss,
but rebels will inhabit a land of fire.

O God, you advanced at your people's head,
as you crossed the desert, the mountains quaked,
the heavens poured rain at the presence of God,
God of Sinai, Israel's God.

Your goodness provided such plentiful rain,
the soil was sterile but you restored it to life;
and there your family found its home,
the place your hands had prepared for the poor.

So bless'd be the Lord while day follows day,
he bears our burdens, the God who saves;
our mighty Salvation delivers us from all,
our God is Lord of the gateways of death.

Now we have seen your processions, O God,
the sacred processions of God our King;
the singers lead, musicians come behind,
girls with tambourines are there in the midst.

Bless God in your choirs, all of Jacob's stem,
Benjamin, last-born, opens the way,
princes of Judah come in their throngs,
the princes of Zebulun, Naphtali's might.

Reveal your power, Lord, summon your might,
the power you show when you take our part;
to the Temple, high on Jerusalem's peak,
great kings draw near, bowed down with gifts.

Rebuke, Lord God, the beast among the reeds,
the throngs of bulls, the nations in herds;
let them swallow their pride and bring silver gifts,
scatter all that delight in war.

From Egypt's land great nobles will come,
Africa will lift up its hands to God;
kingdoms of the world, sing praises to God,
praise the Rider of heaven, of ancient heights;
the sound of his voice is a cry of power,
come, and confess the power of our God!

Over Israel, his splendour, to the heavens, his might
—how awesome is God in his Holy Place;
this is our God, he is Israel's God,
he bestows on his people both strength and power.

Psalm 68 *(Heb. 69)*

I

Antiphon: I am consumed with zeal for your House, O God;
the insults against you fall on me.

Rescue me, O God,
I am about to drown in the flood.

I sink into the slime of the abyss,
where nothing holds firm;
I am swept out to the watery deep,
and drawn beneath the waves.

I am so worn out with shouting
that my throat is on fire;
I have been looking for God,
now my eyes cannot see.

So many detest me without cause,
more than the hairs on my head;
if only I had some of their strength,
they are after my life!

My enemies have forced me to give back
things I did not take;
O God, I will not hide my sins,
my foolishness you know.

Let me not bring disgrace on those who hope,
who trust in God;
they shall not blush for shame as they pray
to Israel's God.

I bear insults for your sake alone,
for you, I am covered with shame;
to my brothers I have become an outcast,
a stranger in my mother's home;
I am consumed with zeal for your House,
the insults against you fall on me.

I humble myself and I fast,
but they make it a cause of reproach;
I put on sackcloth for my clothing,
so they laugh and treat me with scorn,
as they sit at the gates and talk,
while drunkards make me their song.

To you, I lift up my prayer,
make reply, at the hour your choose;
answer soon, for great is your love,
my God, you have promised to save.

II

Antiphon: Draw near, O Lord, and deliver my life,
save me from the hands of my foes.

Pull me out of the swamp, lest I drown,
keep me safe from all of my foes;
save me from the rollers of the deep,
let me not be swept away by the flood;
let me not be engulfed in the pit,
let not the abyss close over my head.

Give me an answer, for kind is your love,
in your compassion, turn and behold;
from your servant, hide not your face,
but consider my distress and send help;
draw near, and rescue my soul,
save me from the hands of my foes.

You know the shame and dishonour I bear,
for my oppressors are all in your sight;
their insults have broken my heart,
my disgrace and despair have no bounds.

I hoped for sympathy, but I found none,
for comforters, not one could I find;
I was hungry, they offered me gall,
with vinegar to quench my thirst. (. . .)

Behold me, in pain and despair,
raise me up by your saving hand;
I will praise the name of God with a song,
proclaiming his glory and love.

The oppressed will see and be glad:
Seekers of God, take heart and live!
The Lord hears the prayer of the captive,
he does not reject those in need;
praise him now, heavens and earth,
give him praise, all the depths of the sea!

For God will come to save Zion,
once again he will build our towns;
and the lands where we dwell shall be ours,
then our children's children's in turn,
a home for all who love God.

Psalm 69 *(Heb. 70)*

Antiphon: O Lord, come to my aid,
my God, save me now!

O Lord, come to my aid,
my God, save me now!
Shame and disgrace on my foes
who would take my life;

How dare they laugh at my pain?
let them scatter in dismay!
How can they bear to jeer at my grief?
Let them flee in shame!

Joy! And glory to our God!
All who seek you are glad;
let them all cry out: Praise the Lord,
all who love your name.

Behold, how helpless I am,
come quickly, my God;
you are my Saviour and my help,
O Lord, do not delay!

Psalm 70 *(Heb. 71)*

Antiphon: My mouth is filled with your praise,
with your glory, all the day long.

To you, O Lord, I turn for help,
I shall never be put to shame;
in your justice, deliver me and save me,
hear my prayer and rescue me, my God.

Give me shelter, stand like a rock,
or a towering wall for my defence;
you alone are my fortress, my rock,
deliver me from the hands of the ungodly,
from the clutches of all evil men.

For in you, O Lord, is my hope,
my Master, my trust since I was born;
you protect me since the day of my birth,
give me help since I came from the womb;
always, you are my praise!

My life has been a challenge for many,
you were always my refuge and defence;
my mouth is filled with your praise,
with your glory all the day long;
never reject me, now that I am old,
do not leave me, though my strength has declined.

My enemies murmur about me,
they conspire and set traps for my life:
God has forsaken him, seize him,
he has no one to come to his aid!
But do not stay away, O Lord,
my God, make haste to help me! (. . .)

My hope, at all times, is in you,
    I will praise you more and more;
my lips will proclaim your justice,
    and your love all day long.

Innumerable are your works, O Lord,
I will sing your justice and power;
O God, since I was young, you have taught me,
so today I announce your great deeds.

Now, I am old and grey-haired,
God, forsake me not!
I will proclaim your glory to all men,
your power and your justice on high;
yes, you have done great things,
God, who is like you?

But you made me feel so much bitter affliction,
you will come once more to restore my strength;
you will come to raise me from the shadows of death
and renew your kindness, to comfort me again.

Now, I will sing praise with the lyre,
    for your faithfulness, my God!
For you, I will play on the harp,
    holiest of Gods!

I will shout for joy as I play,
    for my life is redeemed;
therefore my tongue, all day long
    will sing your great love.

Psalm 71 *(Heb. 72)*

Antiphon: Look up and see, for the Lord is at hand,
the Kingdom and Power are his own.

O God, give your judgement to the King,
make your righteousness his guide;
he will rule your people with right,
and with justice the poor.

Mountains and hills, give your fruit:
his peace on all;
the cause of the poor he will defend,
and deliver those in need.

May he endure as the sun and the moon,
age after age;
he shall come down like rain on the fields,
like showers on the grass.

May justice flourish in his days,
and peace until the end of moons;
may he rule from the sea to the sea,
from the River to distant lands.

Before him desert tribes will bow down,
his foes will lick the dust;
the kings of Tarshish and the isles
bring tribute gifts.

Arabia and Africa send kings,
they offer him gifts;
before him all will bow in awe,
all the nations will serve.

He will rescue the needy when they call,
    he will lift up the poor;
full of pity for the humble and meek,
    he will keep them from death.

From violence and oppression they are safe,
    their blood is precious in his sight!
They will ever be praying for his good,
    May God bless him today!

Abundance of grain on the earth,
    his fame, like the sun;
in him all peoples shall be bless'd,
    they will bless him in turn.

All praise to the Lord, Israel's God,
    he alone does these deeds;
and bless'd be the glory of his name,
    may it cover the earth.

Psalm 72 (extract) *(Heb. 73)*

Antiphon: Lord, you hold me by my right hand,
you will lead me, and bring me to glory.

Yes, to Israel God truly is good,
and to all who are pure of heart. (. . .)
Have I therefore kept my heart pure in vain?
in innocence washed my hands?

For I must suffer day after day,
I am punished at each new dawn;
if I thought: I will speak like your foes,
I would betray the race of your sons.

I tried to understand these things,
but it seemed too difficult for me,
until I came to the Temple of God,
and I considered what is their end.

Suddenly, they fall and are destroyed,
in terror, they are swept away;
like a dream in the morning light,
you wake and their shadows are gone.

Bitter thoughts occupied my heart,
the aching of my wounded soul;
stupid, I would not understand,
I was like some brute in your sight.

But Lord, I shall always stay near you,
you hold me by my right hand;
you lead me by your counsel,
at last you will bring me to glory.

Whom else do I have in heaven?
With you, I desire nothing on earth;
my heart and my flesh may dissolve
but God is for ever my portion, my rock.

It is good to draw close to God,
to take my refuge in the Lord;
now I will tell all your works
at the gates of the Daughter of Zion.

Psalm 73 (extract) *(Heb. 74)*

Antiphon: Be mindful of the oppressed,
whose lives you love.

O God, our King from ancient times,
Author of saving deeds over all the earth;
you divided the sea in the beginning by your might,
you crushed the heads of the dragons in the deep.

There you broke the heads of Leviathan,
you gave him to the beasts of the desert to eat;
then you released the torrents and the springs,
before you brought the dry land from the flood.

Yours is the night, yours also the day,
you fashioned the sun and the moon in their place;
you set the limits that the land must not pass,
winter and summer are the work of your hands.

But remember, Lord, the mocking of your foes,
the insults of godless and foolish men;
save your dove from the vulture's claw,
and be mindful of the oppressed whose lives you love.

Arise, O God, and defend your cause,
remember the mockers who blaspheme you all day;
do not be oblivious to the shouting of your foes,
the uproar of your enemies grows worse every hour.

Consider your covenant, and behold our land,
where violence lurks, at home in every place;
you will not abandon the oppressed to their shame,
the poor and the needy will give thanks for your love.

Psalm 74 *(Heb. 75)*

Antiphon: We call on your name, O Lord,
we proclaim the wonder of your deeds.

We give thanks to you, O God,
we give thanks and we call on your name,
we proclaim the wonder of your deeds.

'When the time has come, I will judge,
I will judge, fairly and with right;
the earth may quake, and all its creatures,
but its pillars I will keep firm.'

'To the boastful, I say: Boast not!
To the impious: Parade not your power!
Parade not your arrogance in the streets,
do not talk with insolence and pride.'

It is neither from the east nor the west,
not the desert, nor the mountain heights,
—no, for God is the judge,
he chastens one, another he exalts.

In the hand of the Lord is a cup,
foaming over with wine, richly spiced;
what he pours must be drunk to the dregs,
all the wicked of the earth must drink.

But I will for ever exult,
I will sing for Jacob's God;
the pride of the sinful will decline,
the heads of the just shall be raised.

Psalm 75 *(Heb. 76)*

Antiphon: God rises up to give sentence,
to save all the oppressed of the earth.

—

In Judah, God is renowned,
in Israel, great is his name;
in Salem, he has fixed his abode,
Zion, the place where he dwells;
there, he broke the swift shafts,
their swords and the shields of war.

Mighty and glorious, you advance,
from the everlasting hills;
the stout-hearted sleep their sleep,
helpless, they were stripped for spoil;
when you rebuked, O God most high,
both chariot and horse lay still.

Lord God, how terrible you are!
Who can stand the fire of your wrath?
You uttered judgement from heaven,
the earth fell silent with fear;
when God rose up to give sentence,
to save all the oppressed of the earth.

The wrath of men becomes your praise,
the survivors will keep your feasts;
make vows, perform them for God,
neighbours, bring gifts to the Lord;
he breaks the spirit of princes,
sends terror to the kings of the earth.

Psalm 76 *(Heb. 77)*

Antiphon: I remember the great deeds of the Lord,
I recall your wonders of old.

With a loud voice, I cry to God,
with a loud voice to God, he will hear.

In the day of my distress, I seek the Lord,
all night long, I stretch out my hands;
my soul will not be consoled,
I remember my God, and I groan,
I ponder, my heart grows faint.

You keep my eyelids from sleep,
I am so troubled that I cannot speak;
I think of the days of old,
and remember the years long ago;
I muse in my heart through the night,
I ponder and my spirit broods:

Will the Lord always reject?
Will his favour return no more?
Has God's kindness utterly ceased,
does his promise no longer hold true?
Has he forgotten his pity and love,
has anger hardened his heart?

And I said: Here is my grief:
the right hand of the Most High has changed!
I remember the great deeds of the Lord,
I recall your wonders of old,
I ponder on all your works
and I muse on your mighty power.

O God, holy are your ways,
what God is great as our God?
You are the God who works wonders,
all the nations have witnessed your power;
you redeemed your people with might,
all Jacob's and Joseph's sons.

The waters saw you, O God,
the waters saw and were in dread;
for the deep of the ocean shook,
and the clouds poured out their flood,
in the sky peals of thunder were heard,
your bright arrows went flashing abroad.

Noise of your thunder pealing out,
your lightning flashed across the world;
the earth trembled and quaked,
your path lay over the seas;
your way stretched across the deep,
the print of your steps was unseen.

You led your people like a flock,
by Moses and Aaron, their guides.

Psalm 79 *(Heb. 80)*

Antiphon: Lord God of hosts, bring us back to you,
have mercy upon us, and we shall all be saved.

Great Shepherd of Israel, hear,
for you guide your people like a flock;
from your cherubim-throne shine forth,
remember the covenant you swore;
rouse up, O God, your might,
and come in your saving power.

Lord God of hosts, bring us back to you,
have mercy upon us, and we shall all be saved.

Lord God of hosts, how long will you delay,
will you be angry with your people's prayer?
You have fed them with a bread of tears,
they have drunk a full draught of tears;
all our neighbours have fought about our land,
all our enemies laugh us to scorn.

Lord God of hosts, bring us back to you,
have mercy upon us, and we shall all be saved.

Once out of Egypt you brought a vine,
to plant it, you swept nations aside;
for it to grow, you cleared the ground,
and it grew, until it covered the land.

The mountains were covered by its shade,
and by its branches the cedars of God;
it grew fronds as far as the sea,
as far as Euphrates' shore.

So why are the walls broken-down?
All who pass can steal away the fruit;
the boars from the forest lay it waste,
it serves as food for the beasts of the field.

Turn back again, Lord God of hosts,
look down from the heavens and see;
visit and take care of this vine,
for your hand once planted its stock;
they have burned it with fire, cut it down,
let them perish at the rebuke of your face.

Give your help to the people of your choice,
this nation you once made so strong;
we will never more turn from your ways,
give us life, and we will call on your name.

Psalm 80 *(Heb. 81)*

Antiphon: Sing out glad songs for God our Strength,
sing and acclaim Jacob's God!

Sing out glad songs for God our Strength,
sing and acclaim Jacob's God.

Raise a song with tambourine-beat,
play music on harps and lyre;
blow trumpets to greet new moons
and full moons, our solemn feasts.

For that is in Israel's Law,
a commandment of Jacob's God;
he gave it to Joseph by decree
as he went out against Egypt's land.

I hear an unknown voice:
I took the burden from your backs,
the baskets fell from your hands;
when you called in distress, I saved.

In the storm I answered you, unseen,
put you to test at the Waters of Strife;
now give heed, my people, to my words,
O Israel, if you would but hear!

In your hearts must reign no other god,
you must worship no other gods;
for I am the Lord your God
who brought you from Egypt's land.

My people would not heed my voice,
and Israel refused to obey;
so I left them in their hardened hearts,
they followed their own stubborn way.

Ah! If my people would hear,
if Israel would walk in my ways!
At once I would conquer their foes,
lifting up against them my hand.

Then the enemies of God would seek grace,
for ever their fate will be sealed;
but I would feed you with the finest wheat,
and fill you with honey from the rock.

Psalm 83 *(Heb. 84)*

Antiphon: See, how my heart is full of longing
for the House of God.

See, how my heart is full of longing
for the House of God.

My soul is pining and sighs
with longing for the House of the Lord;
my heart and my flesh sing: Joy!
to you, O Living God.

For the sparrows have found a house,
and the swallows a nest for their young:
your altar, God of all the worlds,
you, my King and my God.

How bless'd are all who live in your House,
for ever and ever they adore;
happy men, whose strength is in you,
hearts strong for the climb to your throne.

They must go through the Valley of Thorns,
but they find it a place of springs;
they advance from strength to strength,
God will appear to them in Zion.

Lord God, listen to my prayer,
give heed, O Jacob's God;
Lord, our Shield, behold,
and look upon the face of your Christ.

For me, one day in your courts
is better then a thousand elsewhere;
the doorway of the House of my God,
no longer the wicked man's home.

For God is our Sun and our Shield,
he gives us glory and grace;
the Lord refuses no good things
to those whose hearts are true.

Lord of hosts, God almighty,
happy, who trusts in you!

Psalm 84 *(Heb. 85)*

Antiphon: God our Saviour, give us every joy,
and in our orchards harvests of peace.

Your loving-kindness, O Lord, is for your land,
you make the captives of Jacob return;
forgiving your people for their sins,
you pardon their misdeeds of the past;
you restrain all the anger of your wrath,
put an end to the raging of your fury.

Bring us back again, Saviour and God,
forget the bitter grief of your heart;
will you always remember your wrath,
or will your fury persist from age to age?

Will you not come and restore our life again?
That your people may find in you their joy;
show us soon, O Lord, constant love,
grant us once again all your help.

I listen to all that God says,
and the words of God speak of peace,
of peace for his people, his friends,
for all who return with repentance of heart;
surely he will save those who love him,
and his presence will remain in our land.

See, love joins hand in hand with truth,
and peace with justice, arm in arm;
his mercy will reach up from the earth,
and God's righteousness will look down from heaven.

God our Saviour, give us every joy,
and in our orchards harvests of peace;
then justice before God will advance,
preparing the ways of the Lord.

Psalm 85 *(Heb. 86)*

Antiphon: Look upon me, Lord, with your grace,
let your loving mercy abound,
all my life I will trust in your goodness.

Hear my prayer, O Lord, make reply,
for I am poor and in need;
save me from death, since I am your friend,
help the servant whose trust is in you.

You are my God, have mercy, O Lord,
to you I cry all the day;
make the heart of your servant glad,
for to you I lift up my soul.

Master, you are forgiving and good,
when we pray, your kindness abounds;
so listen, O Lord, to my prayer,
attend to the sound of my lament.

In distress, I call on your name,
O Master, you will swiftly reply;
no other god is like you, O Lord,
none can compare with your deeds.

All the nations will come to adore,
O Master, and worship your name;
you are so great, such wonders you do,
you, God, you alone.

Instruct me, Lord, in your ways,
and teach me to walk in your truth;
unite my heart, I will adore.

I give you thanks, Lord God, with all my heart,
for ever I will honour your name;
how great your love towards me has been!
You have saved me from the depths of the grave.

Proud men have risen up in war,
ruthless men have sought my life,
you count for nothing in their sight.

But now, God of mercy and of grace,
slow to anger and steadfast in love;
you remain ever faithful, my Lord,
so turn and have pity on me.

On your servant, bestow your strength,
and save your handmaid's child;
show me soon a sign of your love,
for your help and your comfort are sure.

Psalm 86 *(Heb. 87)*

Antiphon: Glorious things have been said
of the City of God.

She stands high on the sacred hills,
well loved by the Lord;
he cherishes the city of Zion,
more than any other place;
glorious things have been said
of the City of God.

Both Egypt and Babylon I include
among those who obey me;
in Philistia, Africa and Tyre,
the peoples are mine;
for Zion is called Mother by them all,
in her they all belong.

Firmly established, she will stand,
by the hand of the Lord;
as the nations pass by, he records:
Here, this one was born;
In their songs and dances they proclaim:
Here, all have their home!

Psalm 87 *(Heb. 88)*

Antiphon: I call to you, O Lord, every day,
to you I stretch out my hands.

—

Lord my God, I call out by day,
and before you I stand through the night;
let my prayer come to your ears,
hear when I call for help.

For my soul is filled with much pain,
I am poised on the brink of death;
they count me as one for the grave,
I am a man without strength.

Forsaken among the dead,
like the slain lying in their graves;
one of those you no longer recall,
far away from your caring hand.

You have thrown me to the deep of the Pit,
thick shadows in the darkest abyss;
I am crushed by the burdens of wrath,
overwhelmed by its raging waves.

My companions have been frightened away,
the mere sight of me fills them with dread;
from my prison, no way of escape,
for sorrow, my eyes have grown dim.

—

I call to you, O Lord, every day,
to you I stretch out my hands;
did you ever work wonders for the dead?
Do the shades rise up to give praise?

Does the grave declare your great love?
Is your truth proclaimed in the tombs?
Are your wonders admired in the dark,
or your mercy where all is forgotten?

But to you, O Lord, I will cry,
every morning, my prayer rises up;
for what cause did you reject me, Lord?
Why do you hide your face?

In sorrow, dying since my youth,
I am dazed with the burdens of your dread;
your fury has poured over my head,
your terrors laid siege to destroy.

They surround me all the day, like a flood,
on all sides, against me they draw near;
you have thrust back my companions and friends,
my only companion is Night.

Psalm 88 *(Heb. 89)*

Antiphon: The love of the Lord is my song,
he is faithful for ever.

The constant love of the Lord is my song,
my words from age to age announce your truth;
I know: your love is established for all time,
firm as the heavens, you have founded your truth.

You said: I have chosen and sworn by an oath,
with David my servant my covenant is sure;
his descendants shall stand in his place evermore,
for ages to come, his throne shall be preserved.

The heavens give thanks for your marvels, O Lord,
your truth is admired in the gathering of saints;
for who can be compared with the Lord on high,
or who is his equal among the sons of the gods?

God commands awe in the council of the saints,
terrible and great above all in his courts;
Lord God of hosts, who is mighty as you?
Lord of faithfulness, robed in your truth!

It is you that master the surging of the sea,
you that subdue the surging of its waves;
you shattered Rahab and left him dead,
your strength dispersed the armies of your foes.

Yours are the heavens, the earth is your own,
you grounded all the fullness of the world;
the North and the South, that your hand once formed
Hermon and Tabor sing for you in joy.

Sublime is the power, the greatness of your arm,
exalted is your hand, your right hand on high;
your throne is set on justice and right,
your works reveal both kindness and truth.

Glad are the people who raise festal songs,
they will walk in the light of your face;
in your name they rejoice all the day,
they give thanks for your goodness, O Lord.

For you are the glory of our power,
our horn is exalted by your grace;
our shield belongs to our God,
to the Holy One of Israel, our King. (. . .)

Psalm 89 *(Heb. 90)*

Antiphon: The blessings of God be upon us,
Lord, prosper the work of our hands.

—

Lord, you have been our refuge,
from one generation to another!

Before the mountains came forth,
or the face of the earth was made,
from age to age you are God.

You turn us back to the dust,
saying: Return now, children of men!
In your sight, a thousand years are a day,
a day past, one watch of the night.

They are swept away like a dream,
like the morning grass in the fields:
at dawn it springs up and blooms,
by evening, it is withered and dry. (. . .)

So teach us to number our days,
that in wisdom our hearts may grow;
how long still, O Lord? Come soon,
show pity on all who serve.

Fill us each morning with your love,
with your joy and praise, all our days;
for the times of affliction, give joy,
for the years when sadness was our lot.

Let your servants behold your power,
show your glory to those who will come;
the blessings of God be upon us,
Lord, prosper the work of our hands.

Psalm 90 *(Heb. 91)*

Antiphon: I will answer him when he calls,
I am with him in all distress.

All who take shelter in the Lord,
and dwell in the shadow of our God,
may call him: My Fortress, my Shield,
my God in whom is my trust!

And he will free you from the snare,
from the plague that prowls to destroy;
he will shield you with his wings,
in his care, you will be secure.

You will fear no terror in the dark,
nor the arrow that is loosed by day,
no disease that strikes in the night,
nor evils that destroy by day.

Though a thousand fall at your side,
and around you, thousands may die,
you shall stay free of harm,
his faithfulness is ever your shield.

You have only to open your eyes,
you will see what the wicked receive;
but you are my refuge, O God,
I will seek my shelter on high.

Therefore you shall come to no harm,
no scourge will come near your tent;
he has given his angels a command,
they will guard you in all your ways;

they will bear you up in their hands,
lest your foot be hurt by a stone;
you will trample on serpent and lion,
you will triumph over reptile and beast.

If his love is strong, he shall be free,
I will save him, if he knows my name;
I will answer him when he calls,
I am near him in all distress.

I will save him, giving him my praise,
long days shall be his reward,
I will see that he enjoys my peace.

Psalm 91 *(Heb. 92)*

Antiphon: The just flourish like palm trees,
planted in the House of the Lord.

It is good to give thanks to the Lord,
to play for your name, God most high;
to proclaim with the dawn your love,
your truth through the watches of the night;
on the ten-stringed lyre with the lute,
in melodies plucked on the harp.

You have made me glad by your works,
when I see what you have done, I exclaim:
O Lord, how great are your works,
how deep are all your thoughts;
much more than the senseless know,
than the foolish can understand.

The wicked may flourish like the grass,
all evil-doers may thrive,
but see what ruin is their lot,
while the Lord is for ever Most High;
your enemies, Lord, are sure to die,
all the wicked will be destroyed.

You have made me strong like an ox,
upon me you poured out your joy,
my eyes saw the enemy destroyed,
my ears heard the cries of my foes;
but the just will flourish like palm trees,
like Lebanon's cedars they will grow.

They are planted in the House of the Lord,
they spread in the Temple of our God;
even in old age they will bear fruit,
they remain both fresh and strong;
declaring how just is the Lord,
my Rock, in him is no wrong!

Psalm 92 *(Heb. 93)*

Antiphon: God is King, in majesty on high!

God is King, in majesty on high,
our God is girded with might,
he is clothed in garments of power.

The earth stands firm in its place,
unmoved, your throne, from the beginning,
from all time, you are the Lord.

The waters unite in flood,
the waters raise their voice,
the waters thunder and roar.

Greater than the roaring of the sea,
more powerful than the surge of the waves,
the Lord is supreme on high.

Your laws are eternal, O God,
and holiness is the splendour of your House,
for ever and ever, O Lord.

Psalm 93 (extract) *(Heb. 94)*

Antiphon: The Lord himself is my stronghold,
my Rock, my Refuge is God.

Happy are all you instruct, O Lord,
the ones whom you teach by your laws;
you will give them your rest in bad times,
until a pit for the ungodly is dug.

The Lord has not cast off his people,
his inheritance he will not desert;
again the sentence will be just,
it will be followed by the upright of heart.

Against the wicked, who will support me?
Who will stand against those who do wrong?
If the Lord did not come to my aid,
I would soon be in the silent land.

If I say: My foot has slipped,
I am upheld, O Lord, by your love;
when my heart is brimming with cares,
your comfort gives delight to my soul.

You have no part with the unrighteous judges,
they see injustice and call it right;
they pursue the lives of the just
and condemn innocent blood.

The Lord himself is my stronghold,
my Rock, my Refuge is God.

Psalm 94 *(Heb. 95)*

Antiphon: Bow down, let us worship the Lord.

——

Come, shout for joy to the Lord,
and sing to the Rock who saves;
with thanksgiving, come before him,
give praise with music and song.

Great is the Lord, he is God,
a great King above all gods;
in his hands are the depths of the earth,
and the heights of the mountains are his;
his the sea, for he made it,
and the earth, shaped by his power.

Enter in, bend low, bow down,
let us kneel before God our Maker;
for he is our God and we
the people whose Shepherd he is,
the flock he leads with his hand.

Today, if you would hear his voice?
Do not harden your hearts as at the Rock,
on that day of temptation in the desert,
when your fathers tested and proved me,
although they had witnessed my deeds. (. . .)

Psalm 95 *(Heb. 96)*

Antiphon: Joy in heaven, the earth is rejoicing,
in the presence of the Lord, for he comes!

Come, sing to the Lord a new song,
sing to the Lord, all the earth,
sing for him, and bless his name.

Proclaim his salvation day by day,
and tell his glory to the world,
to all peoples his marvellous deeds.

God is great and worthy of all praise,
to be feared above all gods,
the gods of the nations are nought.

It is God who made the heavens,
where glory and majesty attend,
around him beauty and strength.

So praise the Lord, every land,
sing praises for his glory and power,
give praise to the glory of his name.

Bring an offering, enter his House,
worship God in his holy courts,
fall before him, all the earth.

Go, tell the nations: God is King!
Immovable he made the earth,
he will judge the peoples with right.

Joy in heaven, let earth be glad!
Let the sea and its fullness rejoice!
Let the fields with their fruit rejoice,
and the trees of the forest shout for joy

Before the Lord, for he comes,
he is coming to judge the earth;
with justice, he will rule the world,
the peoples he will judge in his truth.

Psalm 96 *(Heb. 97)*

Antiphon: You are, O God, most high,
above all other.

God reigns! Let the earth rejoice,
let the islands of the sea be glad!
Surrounded by darkness and clouds,
he reigns in justice and right.

His vanguard, a consuming fire,
devouring his foes all around;
his lightning speeds across the world,
the earth beholds it in fear.

The mountains flow like wax,
before the Lord of all the earth;
the heavens declare: He is just!
His glory shines in every land.

All who worship idols are disgraced,
their boast is in helpless forms,
all the idols bow down and adore!

Zion gives heed and exults,
the cities of Judah rejoice,
because of your judgements, O Lord.

You alone are Lord,
Most High above all the earth,
in glory above all the gods.

The Lord loves all who hate wrong,
defending the lives of his friends,
he saves them from evil and harm.

A light shall rise on the just,
the upright in heart shall rejoice;
praise God, all who are just,
give thanks, for holy is his name!

Psalm 97 *(Heb. 98)*

Antiphon: Give thanks to God, every nation, Alleluia!
Give praise for the glory of his name, Alleluia!

O sing a new song to the Lord,
for the wonders he has wrought;
for the victory his hand has gained,
his holiness of power.

The Lord has shown that he will save,
in the sight of the nations revealing his power,
ever mindful of his kindness and truth
for the people he loves.

All the ends of the earth have seen
the salvation of our God;
sing out for the Lord, all the earth,
exult in hymns of joy.

Sing praises to God with the harp,
with instruments and songs;
blow high the trumpets and horns,
extol the Lord our King.

Seas and the deep, give voice!
With the world and all its throngs;
let the rivers clap their hands,
all the hills shout for joy!

Before the Lord, for he comes,
he comes to judge the earth,
with justice, he will rule the world,
all peoples, with his truth.

Psalm 98 *(Heb. 99)*

Antiphon: Extol the Lord our God,
holy is the Lord our God!

The Lord is King, the nations tremble,
on cherubim he thrones, the mountains quake,
in Zion, the Lord is King.

He stands on high, above every nation,
they shall glory in his name, filled with awe:
he is God, holy in power.

Most mighty of kings, great lover of right,
you set up equity, throning as the Just,
in Jacob—such are your ways.

Then extol the Lord our God,
fall in worship before his throne:
God, holy indeed!

Moses and Aaron, with Samuel, his priests,
all prayed to the Lord, they invoked his name,
and he, their God, made reply. (. . .)

O Lord, our God, you gave them reply!
You showed them that you are a God who forgives,
although you chastise men for sin.

So extol the Lord our God,
at his Holy Place bow down,
holy is the Lord our God!

Psalm 99 *(Heb. 100)*

Antiphon: Rise up, people of God,
praise him with cymbals and dances!

Give glory to God, all the earth
and worship the Lord with cheerful songs,
go up to him, repeating shouts of joy.

Remember that the Lord is God,
for he made us, the work of his hands,
his people and the sheep of his flock.

So come into his gates, giving thanks,
and enter his courts with songs of praise,
bring him thanks, sing praise to his name.

See, how the Lord is good!
See, for eternity his love!
He is faithful, age after age!

Psalm 100 *(Heb. 101)*

Antiphon: My eyes rest on the faithful in the land,
to keep them near.

Of kindness and judgement I will sing,
your love, O Lord, I will praise;
I will walk in the blameless way,
but when will you come?

I am always blameless of heart,
wherever I dwell;
I have kept before my eyes
nothing base.

I hate the deeds of the doomed,
they shall not be mine;
away with the evil of heart,
I will heed no wrong.

Those who speak secret slander
I will bring down;
the proud of looks and of heart,
I will not endure.

My eyes rest on the faithful in the land,
to keep them near;
if they walk on the blameless path,
they will be my friends.

In my house there is no place
for deceitful hearts;
those who tell lies will not remain
within my sight.

In the morning I will bring down
all the wicked in the land;
I will tear from the City of God
all who love wrong.

Psalm 101 *(Heb. 102)*

Antiphon: All the nations shall honour the Lord,
his splendour all the kings of the earth.

O Lord, consider my prayer,
let my cry come to your ears;
do not hide far from me your face,
in the day when distress is at hand;
incline towards me your ear,
make haste to reply when I call.

For my days drift away like smoke,
my bones, like a bonfire, blaze;
my heart is withered like grass,
I forget to consume my bread;
because I lament without pause,
I am nothing but skin and bones.

Like a bird alone in the desert,
or an owl in a ruined house,
I lie awake and I groan,
like a sparrow lost on a roof;
all day I am mocked by my foes,
in their rage, they call me Accursed.

Ashes are the bread that I eat,
I mingle tears with my drink;
so great are your fury and wrath,
you raised me, then cast me down,
my days are a shadow that wanes,
like the grass, I wither away.

But you, O Lord, for ever you abide,
from age to age your name will endure;
you will arise and have pity on Zion,
it is time for compassion to be shown;
for all who serve you cherish her stones,
moved by her ruins, they weep.

Then all the nations shall honour the Lord,
his splendour, all the kings of the earth;
when the Lord returns to rebuild Zion,
and his glory once again is revealed;
God will consider the prayers of the poor,
he will not despise what they ask.

These things shall be written for the ages to come,
a people not yet born will praise God;
the Lord has looked down from his throne on high,
from heaven he considered the world;
now he has heard the captives' cry,
he has freed those condemned to die.

The sons of your servants will find a home,
their descendants will live in your sight;
in Zion they will declare the name of the Lord,
through Jerusalem, all his praise,
when the peoples gather and come from afar,
all nations will worship the Lord.

On the way, my strength has failed,
and the span of my days is cut short;
do not take me away in mid-course,
you, O Lord, are true for all time.

Of old, you established the earth,
the heavens are the work of your hands;
they will perish, but you endure;
like a garment, all will grow old,
like clothes thrown aside, they will end,
but you remain, no end to your years.

Psalm 102 *(Heb. 103)*

Antiphon: God our Lord is compassion and peace,
rich in patience and mercy, and full of love.

Give praise to the Lord, O my soul,
all my being, praise his holy name,
give praise to the Lord, O my soul,
remember the kindnesses of God.

The Lord will pardon all your misdeeds,
he will heal you of every kind of ill,
he will rescue your life from the grave,
and will crown you with his kindness and love;
he comes to fill you with every kind of good,
and like an eagle, your youth will remain.

For the Lord is a righteous judge,
he brings justice for all the oppressed,
he revealed to Moses his ways,
to the children of Israel his deeds.

The Lord our God is compassion and love,
slow to anger, abounding in concern;
he will not chide us until we despair,
his anger is not destined to endure;
he does not treat us according to our sins,
nor repay us as our ways would deserve.

As high as the sky above the earth,
so the Lord, for all who love him, is kind,
as the east is far from the west,
so far he removes all our sins.

As a father is gentle to his child,
so the Lord, to all who love him, is good;
he knows in what manner we were made,
he remembers that we rose from the dust.

Man! His life is like the grass,
he blossoms like a flower in the fields:
one breath of the wind, he is no more,
and his place will not see him again.

But the love of the Lord for all his friends
is eternal, unending in days;
for the children of their children he is just,
if they keep his covenant and laws,
and take care to fulfil his commands.

The Lord has set his throne in the heavens,
and over all, his kingdom is strong;
give praise to the Lord, all his choirs,
angel-servants, fulfilling his will,
so quick to obey his every word.

Now bless the Lord, all his saints,
faithful ministers, obeying his commands;
give praise to the Lord, all his works,
in all worlds where his majesty is known;
and give praise to the Lord, O my soul.

Psalm 103 *(Heb. 104)*

I

Antiphon: O Lord, my God, you are so great,
robed in light as in a cloak.

Give praise to the Lord, O my soul,
O Lord my God, you are so great,
all clothed in majesty and power,
and robed in light as in a cloak.

You spread out the heavens like a tent,
on the waters, your palaces stand firm;
your chariots are speeding clouds,
you ride on the wings of the wind;
your messengers, a breath of air;
your ministers, a flame of fire.

You founded the earth firm on the rock,
unshaken for ever it will stand;
you clothed it with the garment of the deep,
above the hills, the waters stood high.

Then you rebuked, so the waters fled,
at the thunder of your voice they took flight;
they went leaping over mountains, down vales,
as they sped to the place you had assigned;
then you set them a boundary not to pass,
never again shall they cover the earth.

In the depths of the valleys flow springs,
streams wind at the foot of the hills;
they give drink to the beasts of the field,
wild horses come quenching their thirst;
the birds of the air make their nests,
then perched in the branches, they sing.

From on high you water the hills,
the earth is full of your fruits;
you make grass grow up for the cattle,
many plants to be used by men.

So bread is produced from the earth,
and wine that makes our hearts glad;
there is oil, so that all are content,
and bread so their hearts will grow strong.

Well watered are the trees of the Lord,
the cedars he planted in Lebanon;
the birds build nests in their crowns,
high fir trees are the home of the stork;
in the mountains the wild goats skip,
in clefts of the rock, badgers hide.

II

Antiphon: Give praise to the Lord, O my soul,
O Lord my God, you are so great!

To mark the seasons, you created the moon,
the sun knows at what hour it must set;
then darkness falls, it is night,
when the forest animals roam;
young lions go roaring for prey,
in search of the food God gives.

At sunrise, they creep away,
and return to their dens to sleep;
then man goes out to his work,
he labours till evening draws on.

O Lord, how numerous are your works,
wisely you have accomplished them all;
your creatures cover the earth,
how manifold are your marvels, O God!

There is the sea, so vast and wide,
teeming with incalculable life:
creatures both tiny and large,
above them the ships sail on,
Leviathan gambols and plays.

All look to you, O Lord,
and you give them their food in due time;
whatever you give, they consume,
you open your hand, they are filled.

If you hide your face, they are dismayed,
if you take away their breath, they will die,
returning again to their dust:
you send out your breath, they are made,
you renew the face of the earth.

For ever the glory of the Lord!
Let our Master be glad in his works!
He looks at the earth, and it quakes,
he touches the hills, and they smoke.

All life long, for the Lord I will sing,
while I live, I will praise my God;
may the Lord take pleasure in my words,
since all my joy is in God;
now bless the Lord, O my soul!

Psalm 106 *(Heb. 107)*

I

Antiphon: Give thanks to the Lord, for he is good,
for everlasting is his love.

Give thanks to the Lord, for he is good,
for everlasting is his love:

Such is the hymn of the Lord's redeemed,
those he rescued from the hand of the foe;
whom he gathered from the midst of the lands,
from the East and the West, North and South.

Through the desert and wilderness they strayed,
not finding a town where they could dwell;
starving, they were dying of thirst,
their life was ebbing away.

Then they cried in distress to the Lord,
from their plight he rescued them all;
he led them along straight paths,
until they found a place to dwell.

Let them thank the Lord for his love,
his wonders for the children of men!
He quenched the thirst in their souls,
the hungry, he filled with good things.

Some dwelt in darkness and gloom,
poor prisoners, fettered with chains;
the Most High had seen their misdeeds,
they fell and they found no help.

Then they cried in their distress to the Lord,
from their plight, he rescued them all;
he led them out of darkness and gloom,
and he struck off all their chains.

Let them thank the Lord for his love,
his wonders for the children of men!
He shattered the doors of bronze,
he divided the iron bars.

Some were stricken for their evil ways,
afflicted on account of their sins,
they were sickened of every food,
and stood at the gates of death.

Then they cried in their distress to the Lord,
from their plight, he rescued them all;
he sent out his Word, they were healed,
from destruction he snatched their souls.

Let them thank the Lord for his love,
his wonders for the children of men!
Let them make thank-offerings with praise,
declaring his deeds with shouts of joy.

II

Antiphon: Let us thank the Lord for his love,
his wonders for the children of men!

Some put out to sea in ships,
and traded across the high seas;
they saw the works of the Lord,
his wonderful works in the deep.

He commanded, a great gale arose,
whipping up the waves of the sea;
the ship was borne up, then it plunged,
their hearts were like wax in their breasts.

Reeling, they staggered like men drunk,
all their skills were of no avail;
then they cried in their distress to the Lord,
from their plight, he rescued them all.

He made the storm fall still,
the waves of the sea grew calm;
they rejoiced to be at rest once again,
then he brought them safe to port.

Let them thank the Lord for his love,
his wonders for the children of men!
Let them praise him where the people can hear,
in the council of the elders give praise.

The rivers became dry ground,
their sources no longer flowed;
fruitful land he turned into salt
because of men's evil deeds.

The desert, he changed into lakes,
parched ground became springs and wells,
the hungry he brought there to live,
they established a city as their home.

They sowed fields and planted their vines,
they gathered a fruitful yield;
by his blessings, their number increased,
and their herds suffered no loss.

When they dwindled, brought very low
by oppression, by troubles and pain,
on their foes he poured out contempt,
they were banished to trackless wastes.

But he raised up the poor from their needs,
and their numbers increased like the flocks;
the upright see, and rejoice,
while evil must hold its tongue.

Let the wise consider these things,
who can fathom the love of the Lord?
Give thanks to his name, for he is good,
for everlasting is his love!

Psalm 109 *(Heb. 110)*

Antiphon: The Lord has told my Lord:
You are Prince from the day of your birth.

The Lord has told my Lord:
Sit at my right,
I will make your enemies your footstool.

From Zion, the Lord will stretch forth
your sceptre of power:
Rule over all your foes.

You are Prince from the day of your birth,
on the holy hills,
I begot you like dew before the dawn.

The Lord has sworn without return:
You are for ever a priest,
after the order of Melchizedek. (. . .)

From the wayside brook he will drink,
the Lord your King,
there he will lift up his head.

Psalm 110 *(Heb. 111)*

Antiphon: God nourishes in love all who revere him,
he is the bread of life eternal.

I give thanks to the Lord in my heart,
in the gathered assembly of the just;
great are the works of the Lord,
worthy of study and delight.

Glory and majesty, his works,
and his justice endures evermore,
his marvels we can never forget,
how merciful and gracious is our God!

He gives nourishment to all who revere him,
ever mindful of his covenant and truth;
he reveals to his people his power,
as he gives them the riches of their foes.

His works are faithfulness and truth,
and all his precepts are sure;
for ever and ever they will stand,
received in justice and love.

He has sent his redemption to his people,
he renews his covenant and truth,
holy and almighty is his name.

To honour God is wisdom's concern,
all who obey him are prudent indeed,
for his praise endures evermore.

Psalm 111 *(Heb. 112)*

Antiphon: The just shall never be removed,
his heart stands firm, without fear.

Happy man who honours the Lord,
who delights in obeying his commands;
his descendants shall flourish on the earth,
the household of the just shall be bless'd.

Great wealth and honour in his house,
his dealings will be crowned with success;
for a light shines in the dark
on all who are merciful and just.

It is good to be open and to lend,
to conduct with justice one's affairs;
the just shall never be removed,
they are kept in mind evermore.

He does not fear to receive bad news,
his heart is firm, full of trust,
his heart stands firm, without fear.

He gives help freely to the poor,
and his goodness endures evermore,
his name is respected and loved.

Psalm 112 *(Heb. 113)*

Antiphon: Bow down, let us worship the Lord.

———

Praise, you servants of the Lord,
praise the name of the Lord!
How bless'd is the name of the Lord,
bless'd now, and bless'd evermore!
From the rising to the setting of the sun,
give praise to the name of the Lord!

The Lord reigns over the world,
his glory is exalted on high!
Who can be compared to our God?
Throned in majesty on high,
he looks down upon heaven and earth.

He lifts up the weak from the dust,
from the dunghill he raises the poor,
to give them a seat among the princes,
yes, with the princes of his people;
and he makes the childless woman
happy with children at home.

Psalm 113A *(Heb. 114)*

Antiphon: Baptised in the death of the Lord,
our lives are with him.

When Israel came out of Egypt,
and Jacob from a foreign land,
Judah became His sanctuary
and Israel His domain.

The Red Sea looked and fled,
then Jordan was driven back;
the mountains skipped like rams,
and the hills like young sheep.

O sea, what made you flee?
O Jordan, who turned you back?
Mountains, why skip like rams?
Little hills, like young sheep?

Tremble, earth, before the Lord,
before the face of the God of Jacob,
who turned the rocks into water,
dry stones into a flowing stream.

Psalm 113B *(Heb. 115)*

Antiphon: We, the living, will bless God,
both now and for evermore.

Never to us, O Lord, never to us:
to you alone let glory be given!
On account of your kindness and truth,
lest men ask: Where is your God?

Our God? He is throned on high;
all that he plans, he performs;
while their idols are silver and gold,
all shaped and fashioned by hands . . .

House of Israel, trust in the Lord,
he is both helper and shield!
House of Aaron, trust in the Lord,
he is both helper and shield!

All servants of God, trust in him,
he is both helper and shield!
The Lord will remember and bless us,
he will bless both Israel and Aaron.

He will bless all who honour the Lord,
blessing the small with the great;
May the Lord bless you more and more,
you and your children in turn!

May you be bless'd by the Lord,
the Maker of heaven and earth;
the heavens are the Temple of God,
the earth he has given to men.

So we, the living, will bless God,
both now and for evermore.

Psalm 114 *(Heb. 116A)*

Antiphon: I will walk in the presence of God,
praise him in the land of life.

I love the Lord, for he hears
the sound of my prayer;
he gives heed to me in his love,
whenever I implore him.

The snares of death closed around,
all the horror of the grave;
I was plunged in doubt and despair,
till I called the name of God.

For the Lord is compassionate and good,
yes, our God is just;
with his hand he defends the poor,
when I slipped, he saved my life.

Return then, my soul, to your rest,
for you know the Lord is good;
he has saved my soul from death,
and my life from defeat.

I will walk in the presence of God,
praise him in the land of life.

Psalm 115 *(Heb. 116B)*

Antiphon: Very dear in the eyes of the Lord
is the death of every friend.

I believed, even when I said:
Too great is the pain!
In my grief, I nearly said:
Every man is but a liar!

Then what can I offer to the Lord
for the goodness he has shown?
I will lift high Salvation's cup,
I will praise his holy name.

Very dear in the eyes of the Lord
is the death of every friend;
I will serve as my mother served,
you struck off all my chains.

I will offer a sacrifice of praise,
I will call on your name;
I will walk in the presence of God,
praise him in the land of life.

I will perform my vows to the Lord,
while his servants stand around;
in the courts of the House of the Lord,
in your midst, Jerusalem.

Psalm 116 *(Heb. 117)*

Antiphon: All nations of the world,
give praise to the Lord!

Every nation, praise the Lord: Alleluia!
And all peoples, praise his name: Alleluia!
For his love towards us is strong: Alleluia!
To his faithfulness, no end: Alleluia!

Psalm 117 *(Heb. 118)*

Antiphon: This day is the day of the Lord,
let us rejoice and be glad!

Give thanks to the Lord, he is good,
for everlasting is his love.

Let the house of Israel proclaim:
Everlasting is his love!
Let the house of Aaron proclaim:
Everlasting is his love!
Let the God-fearing all proclaim:
Everlasting is his love!

In distress, I called to the Lord,
he heard me, he set me free;
the Lord is with me, fear not!
What harm can people do?
With the Lord at my side to help,
I shall conquer my foes.

It is better to take refuge in God,
than to trust in a man;
it is better to take refuge in God,
than to trust in a prince;
all the nations gathered around,
I conquered by the name of the Lord.

Hard-pressed, I was almost at an end,
but the Lord came to my aid;
God is my strength and my song,
for he saved my life;
joyful, the victory-songs
in the tents of the just.

The right hand of the Lord does wonders,
how glorious, his strength!
I shall not die, I shall live,
and proclaim the works of God;
he chastened me time after time,
but never abandoned my soul.

Open wide his Justice-gates,
I will give thanks to the Lord;
this is the Gate of the Lord,
the just shall enter in;
I give thanks, for I have been heard,
he has exalted my soul!

The stone which the builders refused
is now the key-stone;
this is the work of the Lord,
a great wonder in our eyes;
this day is the day of the Lord,
let us rejoice and be glad!

Lord, bestow your salvation,
give us new life!
Blessed is he who comes
in the name of the Lord!
We bless you from the House of God,
the Lord our God is our light.

Form processions, with branches in hand,
come to the altar of God;
for you are my God, I give thanks,
O God, I adore!
Give thanks to the Lord, he is good,
for everlasting is his love!

Psalm 118 *(Heb. 119)*

I

Antiphon: In the way of your testimonies is my joy,
more than in boundless wealth.

———

How happy are all without fault,
who walk in God's laws;
and happy they who pursue his commands,
who seek him with all their heart.

No evil is found in their lives,
for they walk in his ways;
Lord, you laid down your decrees
to be kept without fail.

If only my feet can stay firm
in pursuit of your will;
for then I shall not be ashamed,
if I observe your commands.

I will praise you in purity of heart,
as I see how you judge;
I resolve to obey all your laws,
abandon me not, O Lord.

———

How can a youth remain pure?
If he keeps your commands.
My whole heart has sought for your ways,
do not take your law away.

In my heart I have kept all your laws,
I will not fail in your sight;
how bless'd is your name, O Lord,
instruct me in your ways.

My lips will repeat aloud
    all the judgements of your lips;
in the way of your testimonies is my joy,
    more than in boundless wealth.

Your precepts are the centre of my thoughts,
    I examine your decrees;
I find such delight in your commands,
    your commandments I ever recall.

II

Antiphon: Open my eyes and I will see
    the wonders of your law.

Be good for your servant and I will live,
    I will keep your decrees;
open my eyes and I will see
    the wonders of your law.

A pilgrim I am on the earth,
    do not hide your commands;
with longing, my soul is consumed,
    with desire for your decrees.

You rebuke the proud, they are dismayed,
    for they neglect your commands;
deliver me from their insults and contempt,
    I have kept all your ways.

Though the rulers take counsel to kill,
    I pursue your decrees;
in your testimonies I find great delight,
    in them alone good advice.

My life lies bruised in the dust,
    revive me by your word;
I consider my deeds, you are near,
    so teach me your will.

Expound all the paths of your law,
    your wonders I pursue;
in sorrow, my soul is perplexed,
    by your words give me strength.

Turn my feet aside from false paths,
    in your goodness instruct me;
I have chosen to follow your truth,
    in your judgements I delight.

I stay close to your precepts, O Lord,
    let me not be put to shame;
I make haste to obey your commands,
    you will widen my heart.

III

Antiphon: Guide me in the way of your commands,
    for there alone is my joy.

Teach me, Lord, the sense of your laws,
    I will obey them always;
explain, and I will observe your decrees,
    I will keep them with all my heart.

Guide me in the way of your commands,
    for there alone is my joy;
incline my heart to fulfil your will,
    and not towards wealth.

Preserve my eyes from things of no worth,
renew me according to your word;
keep the promise you made to me of old,
as to all who love your word.

Deliver me from the insults I fear,
for your judgements are good;
see, I desire your commands,
give me life, you are just.

Reveal your great love, O Lord,
your salvation that you swore;
to their insults I will answer with truth,
since I trust in your word.

Never rob me of your truthful word,
for your judgements are my hope;
at all times I will observe your law,
in the ages still to come.

Set me free to pursue my course,
I have sought your decrees;
of your testimonies I will speak before kings,
and will not be ashamed.

Your commands are the source of delight,
I love them with great love;
at your commandments I lift up my hands,
I will ponder your decrees.

IV

Antiphon: In my torment, my soul was consoled,
since your promises give life.

Remember your words to your servant,
you renewed me in hope;
in my torment, my soul was consoled,
since your promises give life.

The proud have beaten me about,
but I never left your law;
I remember your judgements of old,
I am comforted, O Lord.

I am full of rage to see them do wrong,
for they abandon your ways;
I make songs of all your decrees,
here in exile on earth.

I remember your name in the night,
I consider your law;
my happiness lies in one thing:
obeying your commands.

You are all my desire, O Lord,
I will keep your commands;
I beseech you with all my heart,
have mercy as you have sworn.

I reflect on the way that I live,
I will follow your decrees;
I will hasten and not delay,
to conform to your will.

The wicked lay traps for my life,
    I forget not your law;
I rise at midnight to give thanks,
    for your judgements are just.

I am close to all who adore you,
    who keep your laws;
your love, O Lord, fills the earth,
    teach me your decrees.

V

Antiphon: If you show your goodness, I shall live,
    for your law is my delight.

To your servant, Lord, you are good,
    your promises are sure;
teach me to be sensible and wise,
    for I trust your commands.

Before I was afflicted, I went astray,
    now I obey your word;
how good you are, and how kind,
    teach me your commands.

I am snared by the lies of the proud,
    my heart remains true;
their minds cannot understand this:
    I have joy in your law.

My afflictions have done me much good,
    I have learned your decrees;
how precious is the law of your lips,
    more than millions in silver or gold!

By your hands I was fashioned and made,
give me knowledge of your law;
when they see, your people will be glad,
in your promises I trust.

I know, your judgements are right,
I am troubled, you are just;
may your love be for ever my comfort,
as your servant once heard.

If you show your goodness, I shall live,
for your law is my delight;
the proud bear false witness, to their shame,
I will keep your decrees.

Let your friends come near to me now,
all who know your commands;
my heart will be perfect in your ways,
I will not be put to shame.

VI

Antiphon: I am yours, save me, O Lord,
I pursue your commands.

My soul is longing for your salvation,
my trust is in your word;
my eyes look for your promise in vain,
I wonder, will you come?

I was nothing but a wineskin in the smoke,
yet I did not forget;
how long must your servant still wait?
Will my oppressors be repaid?

Proud men have dug pits for my feet,
    they challenge your law;
save me, Lord, your commandments are true,
    men torture me with lies.

They have almost destroyed me on earth,
    but I keep your commands;
restore me, on account of your love,
    that I may follow your laws.

Everlasting, O Lord, are your words,
    eternal in the heavens;
for age after age, your truth,
    you founded the earth to endure.

All things remain by your will,
    by them all you are served;
if your law had not been my delight,
    I would have perished for grief.

I will never forget what you taught,
    you have kept me alive;
I am yours, save me, O Lord,
    I pursue your commands.

Though the wicked lie in wait for my soul,
    I will ponder your laws;
I have seen: all things have an end,
    your will alone endures.

VII

Antiphon: Your commands are my inheritance for ever,
they are the joy of my heart.

How I love your law, O Lord God,
I observe it all day long;
your commandments are always at hand,
I grow wiser than my foes!

More than all my masters, I understand,
since I ponder your law;
in discernment I excel any sage,
for I keep your commands.

I will shun every path of wrong,
and I long to keep your words;
I will not neglect your decrees,
since they come from your hand.

Your testimony is sweet on my lips,
like honey on my tongue;
by your precepts, intelligence is mine,
I detest every way of lies.

Your Word is a lamp on my path,
and a light for my steps;
I have sworn and will keep my oath:
I will observe your just laws.

My sufferings are terrible indeed,
give me life by your Word;
accept the prayers that I bring,
and teach me your commands.

My life is in peril all day long,
    I remember your law;
for my soul, the wicked lay a trap,
    I will obey your decrees.

Your commands are my inheritance for ever,
    they are the joy of my heart;
I am firmly resolved to obey,
    for an eternal reward.

VIII

Antiphon: Hold me, I will be safe with you,
    my eyes fixed on your commands.

I detest men divided of heart,
    but your law I love;
Lord, my defender and shield,
    in your words I trust.

Away from me, sinful men!
    I will obey God's commands;
uphold me as you promised, I shall live,
    do not disappoint me in my hope.

Hold me, I will be safe with you,
    my eyes fixed on your commands;
you abandon those who turn from your law,
    too foolish in their deceit.

The godless are removed from the earth,
    so I love what you teach;
I tremble with awe before your face,
    your judgements fill me with fear.

I have done what is righteous and good,
    save me from those who kill;
Lord, swear that your servant will be safe,
    stop the wickedness of the proud.

My eyes yearn to see your salvation,
    the justice that you swore;
defend now your servant in your love,
    and teach me your commands.

I am your servant, let me understand,
    and tell me your will;
it is time, Lord, now you must act,
    for your law is not obeyed.

I love your commands more than gold,
    than the finest gold;
therefore I adhere to your law,
    and I hate the way of lies.

IX

Antiphon: To your servant reveal your face,
    instruct me in your laws.

How wonderful are all your decrees,
    I will obey every one;
as your Word is revealed, it gives light,
    and the simple understand.

Open-mouthed, I thirst for your commands,
    so great is my desire;
turn towards me, have mercy in your love,
    show justice to your friends.

As you promised, make my steps sure,
keep wrong-doing far away;
deliver me from those who oppress,
I will obey your commands.

To your servant reveal your face,
and instruct me in your laws;
my eyes are streaming with tears,
since they will not keep your laws.

How righteous you are, O Lord!
How just in your ways!
You lay down the demands of your truth,
with faithfulness and love.

My zeal is aflame in my breast,
my foes ignore your commands;
your promises survive every trial,
so your servant holds them dear.

Downcast I am and despised,
but your precepts I recall;
your justice is eternal and right,
there is truth in your law.

I am broken with trouble and distress,
but your decrees bring me joy;
your message is just in every age,
I understand and I shall live.

X

Antiphon: I lie awake all night long,
and think of your laws.

I call with my whole heart, give heed,
I will keep your commands;
I call: save me, O Lord,
I will observe your law.

I implore your aid before the dawn,
I put my trust in your words;
I lie awake all night long,
and think of your laws.

In your mercy and love, hear my prayer,
by your justice give me life;
wrong-doers are gathering around,
they are far from your law.

But you are close, O my Lord,
there is truth in your commands;
long ago I learned of your laws:
that they are sure to endure.

Consider my pain and set me free,
for I did not forget your law;
defend my cause and send me help,
as you promised, give me life.

Your salvation is far from wicked men,
they have no care for your laws;
but great is your compassion, O Lord,
by your justice, give me life.

How many are my rivals and my foes!
Yet I keep your commands;
I feel ashamed when I see them betray,
they will not keep your commands.

See how I love your decrees,
by your mercy give me life;
truth is the foundation of your law,
your righteous judgements never fail.

XI

Antiphon: No, I did not forget your commands,
let my soul have life for your praise.

Great princes have pursued me for no cause,
but my heart will keep your Word;
joy in your promise for my soul,
as on finding hidden gold.

I hate and detest every lie,
and I cleave to your law;
seven times a day I give you thanks,
all your judgements are true.

Great peace for all who love your law,
they cannot be brought down;
I wait for your salvation, O Lord,
I live by your commands.

All that you have taught, I observe,
for therein is my love;
I obey your precepts and commands,
all my deeds are in your sight.

Let my tears have value in your sight,
    give me wisdom by your Word;
let my prayer come before your face,
    save my life as you have sworn.

My lips will ever give you praise,
    for you teach me your will;
my tongue will sing of your decrees,
    all your orders are sure.

Stretch out your hand, give me help,
    I have chosen your commands;
I long for your salvation, O Lord,
    in your law is my delight.

Let my soul have life for your praise,
    may your judgements be my help;
I am astray, a sheep that is lost,
    come in search of my soul.

Psalm 119 *(Heb. 120)*

Antiphon: In my distress, I prayed and called to the Lord,
then he replied.

In my distress, I prayed to the Lord,
I called and he replied;
Lord, save me from the lies of their lips,
from the deceit on their tongues.

Now what shall he give as your reward,
you treacherous tongues?
An archer's sharp arrows, perhaps,
or embers from the hearth?

For too long now my soul has lived
where people hate peace;
my desire is for peace, but if I speak,
they make ready for war.

Psalm 120 *(Heb. 121)*

Antiphon: All my help will come from the Lord
who made both heaven and earth.

I lift up my eyes to the hills,
where shall I look for help?
All my help will come from the Lord,
who made both heaven and earth.

He will not let you stumble or fall,
your guardian will not sleep;
No, the Guardian of Israel
never falls asleep.

The Lord is your Guardian and your shield,
he will stay close at hand;
the sun will not strike you by day,
nor the moon in the night.

The Lord will keep you from all harm,
he will guard your soul;
he will guard you as you come and go,
both now and evermore.

Psalm 121 *(Heb. 122)*

Antiphon: O what joy as I made my way
up to the House of the Lord!

I was glad when they said: Let us go
to the House of the Lord;
and now we have stayed our steps
in Jerusalem's gates.

Jerusalem! Built as a city,
one, unified whole!
The tribes go up to her gates,
all the tribes of the Lord.

To give thanks to the name of the Lord,
for such is his command,
in the place where his justice is throned
since David was king.

So pray that Jerusalem has peace:
Peace upon your friends!
May peace be seen in your walls
and peace in your homes.

For the sake of my brothers and my friends,
I will pray for your peace;
for the sake of the House of the Lord,
I will pray that you be bless'd.

Psalm 122 *(Heb. 123)*

Antiphon: To you, Lord, I lift up my eyes,
when will you come to my aid?

To you I lift up my eyes,
as you throne on high;
my eyes, like a slave's, intent
on his master's hand;

or like the eyes of a maid
on her mistress's hands:
so our eyes are fixed on the Lord,
until his mercy is revealed.

Have mercy on us, Lord, in your love,
we are despised far and wide;
too long have we been despised
and scorned by the proud.

Psalm 123 *(Heb. 124)*

Antiphon: Like birds, our souls flew away
from the fowler's net.

If the Lord had not been on our side
—let Israel now say—
if the Lord had not been on our side
when they rose to attack,
they would surely have swallowed us whole,
so inflamed was their rage.

The waters would have swept us away,
overwhelmed by the flood;
the waves would have covered our heads,
the storm-tossed waves;
so bless the Lord! We were not left
as prey in their grasp.

Like birds, our souls flew away
from the fowler's net;
the snare was broken and torn,
so now we are free!
Our help is in the name of the Lord,
who made heaven and earth.

Psalm 124 *(Heb. 125)*

Antiphon: Happy are they who trust in the Lord,
they cannot be moved, for ever they abide.

Those who trust in the Lord are like Mount Zion,
it cannot be moved, for ever it abides.

As Jerusalem is hedged round with hills,
so the Lord embraces his flock,
both now and for evermore.

A scepter of evil shall not remain
in the land of the just;
lest the just be tempted to turn
their hands to wrong.

Do good, O Lord, to the good,
to all the upright of heart.
May Israel see peace!

Psalm 125 *(Heb. 126)*

Antiphon: All who went in tears and sorrow
return with shouts of joy!

When the Lord brought our prisoners home,
it felt like a dream!
Every mouth was filled with laughter,
and our lips with songs!

In other lands, people said: What wonders
the Lord has done for them!
The Lord has done marvels indeed,
how great is our joy!

Bring back our captives, O Lord,
like streams after rain;
then the sowers who sowed in tears
will harvest in joy.

They went out with sobbing and tears
when the seed was sown;
now they come with laughter and with songs,
for the sheaves are gathered!

Psalm 126 and **127** (extract) *(Heb. 127 and 128)*

Antiphon: From his courts, the Lord send you bliss,
every day of your life.

If the house is not built by the Lord,
the builders will labour in vain;
if a city is not guarded by the Lord,
the guards keep watch in vain.

You rise from sleep early in vain,
and go to rest late, in vain,
you consume the dry bread of your toil
while the Lord feeds his flock as they sleep.

You are happy, revering the Lord,
pursuing his commands;
you shall enjoy the fruit of your hands,
happily, favoured indeed!

From his courts, the Lord send you bliss,
every day of your life;
you shall see how your children grow,
and flourish in peace.

Psalm 128 *(Heb. 129)*

Antiphon: The Lord has done marvels indeed,
how great is our joy!

They have been after me since I was young,
—Israel may say—
they have been after me since I was small,
but they never brought me down!

The plowers ploughed on my back,
their furrows were long!
But the Lord has destroyed—he is just—
all the cords of their snares.

Let them be ashamed and turn back,
all the rivals of Zion;
let them be like grass on the roof,
dried up before it can grow;

with no one to harvest the seed
or to gather the sheaves;
and no passers-by to exclaim:
You are bless'd by the Lord!

Psalm 129 *(Heb. 130)*

Antiphon: I hope in the Lord with all my heart,
I am eager for his Coming.

From the depths I cry to you, O Lord,
give heed to my lament;
let your ear be attentive and hear
the sound of my calling.

If you remember, O Lord, all our faults,
who then can survive?
But with you our pardon is sure,
and therefore we adore you.

My soul is eager for the Lord,
I trust his every word;
my soul is more eager for the Lord
than a watchman for the dawning.

With the Lord is tenderness and love,
his compassion overflows;
so Israel will be saved by the Lord
from all of their failings.

Psalm 130 *(Heb. 131)*

Antiphon: Put your hope in the Lord,
both now and evermore.

O Lord, my heart is not proud,
my eyes are not harsh;
I am not intent on great things
or achievements sublime.

No, my soul lies at rest,
as quiet as a child;
my soul is as still as a babe
at its mother's breast.

Put your hope in the Lord,
both now and evermore.

Psalm 131 *(Heb. 132)*

Antiphon: I will give you a King of David's line,
he shall be crowned with endless glory.

Remember David, O Lord,
how great all the hardships he endured;
recall the oath he swore to his God,
the vow made to Jacob's Might:

'I will not enter the house where I live,
nor lie down on the couch where I sleep,
my eyes shall not take any rest,
not one moment my eyelids shall close,
until I find a place for my Lord,
a home for Jacob's God.'

You see, in Ephratha we heard:
out in the fields of the forest it was found!
Let us enter, go in where he dwells,
bow down before his throne and adore!

Now arise to your resting-place, O Lord,
you and the Ark of your Might;
may your priests be decked in righteous deeds,
let the faithful cry out and rejoice;
for your servant, for David's sake,
reject not your chosen king.

To David the Lord once swore,
an oath which he will not forget:
A son of your own will be king,
I will set him after you on the throne.

If your sons observe my commands,
if they keep the decrees I have taught,
then their sons in turn, evermore,
shall inherit the throne which was yours.

For Zion is the choice of the Lord,
he has chosen to make it his home:
Here is the place where I will rest,
here I will dwell, such is my will.

I will bless her with abundance of corn,
her poor I will satisfy with bread;
with salvation her priests shall be robed,
all her faithful shall sing and be glad.

I will raise up David's descent,
I will set there a lamp for the King;
I will cover his enemies with shame,
on his brow the diadem will shine.

Psalm 132 and **133** (extracts) *(Heb. 133 and 134)*

Antiphon: Come, give praise to the Lord,
all you servants of our God.

See, how pleasant it is, and good,
when brothers and sisters are one!

It is dew on the heights of Hermon,
descending on Zion,
the blessing of the Lord is there,
and eternal life.

Come, give praise to the Lord,
all you servants of our God;
as you stand in the House of the Lord,
by night in the courts of our God.

In his Temple, lift up your hands,
in deep night, sing praise to our God;
may the Lord bless you from Zion,
the Maker of heaven and earth.

Psalm 134 *(Heb. 135)*

Antiphon: All that God wills, he performs,
in heaven, on earth, in the deep.

Give praise to the name of the Lord,
exult, you servants of God!
As you stand in the House of the Lord,
in the courts of the House of our God!

Sing praise to the Lord, he is good,
give praise to his name, he is kind;
for Jacob was the Chosen of God,
and Israel he has made his Own.

I know how great is our God,
our Saviour above all gods!
For all that he wills, he performs,
in heaven, on earth, in the deep.

Clouds race from the ends of the earth,
while lightning and rain lash down,
from his storerooms he brings wild storms . . .

He performed his wonders and signs
far away in Egypt's midst;
then he gave a promised land
to Israel whom he chose in his love.

Your name, O Lord, evermore!
Your renown, O God, never fades!
For our Lord is our strong defence,
to his servants, the Lord is good.

Other nations have idols of gold,
all fashioned by human hands:
they have mouths but they do not speak,
their eyes are unable to see!

With their ears no word can be heard,
no breath will pass through their lips;
so shall be all who make them,
with those who believe in their power.

House of Israel, give praise to the Lord!
House of Aaron, give praise to the Lord!
House of Levi, give praise to the Lord!
All believers, give praise to the Lord!

Psalm 135 *(Heb. 136)*

Antiphon: God alone performed mighty deeds,
to all flesh in compassion he gives bread.

Offer thanks to the Lord, for he is good!
—He is our God, love without end!
Offer thanks to the Lord, the God of Gods!
—He is our God, love without end!
Offer thanks to the Lord of all Lords!
—He is our God, love without end!

He alone performed mighty deeds!
—He is our God, love without end!
His hands with wisdom made the heavens!
—He is our God, love without end!
He set the dry land in the seas!
—He is our God, love without end!

He created the givers of light,
—he is our God, love without end!
The sun that thrones upon the day,
—he is our God, love without end!
The moon and the stars that rule the night,
—he is our God, love without end!

He divided the ocean in two parts,
—he is our God, love without end!
And led his people to the shore,
—he is our God, love without end!
But Pharaoh and his army he destroyed,
—he is our God, love without end!

Through the desert his people he brought,
—he is our God, love without end!
He struck mighty kings for their sake,
—he is our God, love without end!
He felled mighty princes for our sake,
—he is our God, love without end!

All their lands to our fathers he gave,
—he is our God, love without end!
their pastures he intended for our flocks,
—he is our God, love without end!
He saved us in all our despair,
—he is our God, love without end!

He has freed us from the hands of our foes,
—he is our God, love without end!
To all flesh in compassion he gives bread,
—he is our God, love without end!
So give thanks to the Lord God of Heaven!
—He is our God, love without end!

Psalm 136 *(Heb. 137)*

Antiphon: In our sorrow we laid our harps aside,
for God's House was far away.

Beside the rivers in Babylon
we fell down and we wept
as our thoughts turned to Zion;
high on the branches of the trees
we abandoned our harps.

And there we were asked
by our captors for songs,
by our jailers for joy:
Sing us now, they would say,
one of Zion's holy songs.

How could we bear to sing
a song of the Lord
in a land not our own?
If I forget Jerusalem
let my right hand be consumed.

I would rather that my tongue
should cleave to my lips
if ever I forgot:
if Jerusalem is less
than the highest of my joys.

Psalm 137 *(Heb. 138)*

Antiphon: I will make songs for the Lord,
let his angels adore!

I give you thanks, O Lord, with all my heart:
you have heard the words of my mouth;
in the presence of angels I will sing,
towards your temple I will bow down.

I give you thanks for your kindness and your truth,
all your promises excell your renown;
when I called, you answered my prayer,
you increased the strength of my soul.

All the kings of the earth will give you praise,
for they have heard the words of your mouth;
they shall sing of the ways of the Lord:
Great is the glory of the Lord!

God is high, yet the humble he beholds,
the proud he sees from afar;
though I walk in the midst of distress,
my life is safe from the fury of my foes.

I stand firm, by the actions of his love,
all his promises the Lord will fulfil;
to your mercy, O Lord, there is no end,
so continue the work you have begun.

Psalm 138 *(Heb. 139)*

Antiphon: The darkest night is no longer dark at all,
the deepest shadow will become bright as day.

O Lord, you have fathomed me and know me,
you know if I sit down or stand,
you follow my thoughts from afar.

You watch as I work and as I rest,
how familiar to you are all my ways!
Before ever a word is on my tongue,
you know it entirely, O Lord!

You surround me, behind and before,
your hand is upon me with power:
such knowledge is too deep for me to bear,
too lofty for me to attain.

So where can I escape from your Spirit?
From your presence where can I flee?
If I go up to heaven, you are there,
if I lie in the tomb, you are near.

If I take the wings of the dawn,
and reside on a distant shore,
there too your hand is my guide,
your right hand still holds me fast.

If I say: I will hide in the dark,
let the light around me be night;
then the darkness for you is not dark,
and the night is as clear as the day.

You created my inmost parts,
as you wove me within the womb;
I give thanks, for the mystery is great:
what wonders all your works reveal!

You know full well, my soul:
all my bones were not unknown,
while secretly I was formed
and fashioned in the depths of the earth.

You saw me before I was born,
and my days were inscribed in your book:
they were all decided and set
before even one came to be!

How precious are your thoughts, O God,
how vast are all your designs!
In number they are more than the sand;
I may dream, but still you remain. (. . .)

Examine me, O God, explore my heart,
test my thoughts, discover my mind;
inspect me for evil within
and guide me to eternal paths.

Psalm 139 *(Heb. 140)*

Antiphon: O God, my Master, my Saviour and Strength,
in the battle you cover my head.

———

Save my life, O Lord, from wicked men,
preserve me from violent hands;
from those whose hearts devise evil deeds,
who stir up disputes all day long;
they sharpen their tongues like a deadly snake's,
viper's venom is upon their lips!

Protect me from the hands of the wicked, O Lord,
save me from violent men;
those who have plans to make me fall,
they stretch out a cord for my feet;
to catch me, proud people have hidden a trap,
along my path, their snares are concealed.

To the Lord, I say: But you are my God!
So hear my voice when I plead;
O God, my Master, my Saviour and Strength,
in the battle you cover my head;
O Lord, grant not what the wicked desire,
their plans must never succeed. (. . .)

I know that the Lord will give justice and right,
he is good to the afflicted and poor;
yes, the just will give thanks to your name,
the upright will live in your sight.

Psalm 140 *(Heb. 141)*

Antiphon: Like incense, my prayer rise up in your sight,
and my hands like an offering by night.

O God, hear my prayer, make haste to my help!
Pay heed to my voice when I call on your name;
like incense, my prayer rise up in your sight,
and my hands like an offering by night.

Set a watch, O Lord, at the gate of my lips,
let a guard be posted before my tongue;
let my heart be inclined to no evil ways,
nor engage in mischief with those who do wrong.

No, I will never partake of their delights,
if a just man strikes or reproves me, it is good;
but the unction of the wicked I will sternly reject,
no matter what they do, I will continue to pray.

Their judges are cast down! They fell from the crag
when they heard how gracious my words could be;
like a rock that is split and shattered in the field,
their bones lie strewn on the edge of the Pit.

To you, O Master, I lift up my eyes,
with you I seek refuge, deliver my life!
Save me from the nets and the snares they have laid,
I will pass by the traps of the wicked unscathed.

Psalm 141 *(Heb. 142)*

Antiphon: In the land of the living,
the Lord is my all!

I call to the Lord for help,
I plead with the Lord in loud cries;
I pour out before him my complaint,
I lay bare my distress in his sight;
within me, my spirit grows faint:
but you know full well all my ways.

On the path along which I walk
my foes have concealed a trap;
when I look around me, I see
there is not one who pays heed!
I have no hope of escape,
since no one is concerned for my life.

I call out to you, O Lord,
I say: Lord, my Defence!
In the land of the living, my All!
Give heed to the sound of my prayer,
for now I am brought to despair.

Save me from the men who pursue,
since they are too strong for me;
deliver my soul from distress,
that I may give thanks to your name;
then the just will gather around,
we will praise your goodness, O Lord.

Psalm 142 *(Heb. 143)*

Antiphon: Show me the way to go,
for to you I lift up my soul.

O Lord, give heed to my prayer,
and listen to the sound of my plea;
you are faithful and good, make reply,
put not your servant on trial,
for no one is just in your eyes.

The enemy is in pursuit of my soul,
he has crushed my life to the ground,
he has left me alone in the dark,
like those already long dead;
my breath within me is faint
and my heart is shaking with dread.

I remember the days of old,
and I ponder on all your works;
I consider the wonders of your hands
and I lift up my heart to you,
I thirst for you with all my soul.

Make haste to answer, O Lord,
for I have lost all hope;
hide not your face from me,
lest I become like those in the Pit.

Let me hear of your love at dawn,
for in you is my trust;
show me the way to go,
for to you I lift up my soul.

Save me from my enemies, O Lord,
as my hope is in you;
teach me to follow your will
since you are my God;
the goodness of your Spirit be my guide:
lead me to level ground.

For the sake of your name, O Lord,
in your justice set me free;
deliver my soul in distress,
for you alone I will serve.

Psalm 143 *(Heb. 144)*

Antiphon: You are bless'd, O Lord, my Rock,
my Shield in whom I can trust!

——

You are bless'd, O Lord, my Rock!
He trains my hands for the fight,
makes ready my fingers for war.

My companion he is, and my defence,
my stronghold, the One who can save,
my shield in whom I can trust,
the nations are subdued by his might.

What is man that you heed him, O Lord?
The child of man, that you care?
For he is nothing more than a breath,
his days are a fleeting shade.

Incline your heavens and come down,
touch the mountains and they will smoke,
flash lightning and put them to flight,
shoot arrows and make them disperse.

Stretch out your hand from on high
and snatch me from the terrible flood;
to my God, I will sing a new song,
I will sing for his praise with the lyre.

Psalm 144 *(Heb. 145)*

Antiphon: I proclaim your greatness, O God,
I will bless your name evermore!

—

I proclaim your greatness, O God,
I will bless your name evermore.

I long to praise you every day,
I will bless your name evermore;
God is great and highly to be praised,
in his glory beyond compare.

Every age will praise you for your deeds
and will tell the coming age of your might;
of your splendour and glory they will speak,
I will ponder the wonder of your deeds.

They admire the power of your hands,
while I exclaim: How great is our God!
They boast of the Lord in his love,
acclaiming your kindness with joy.

The Lord is merciful and good,
slow to anger, abounding in love;
the Lord is bounteous to all,
he has compassion on all that he has made.

All your creatures, Lord, give you thanks,
let your friends recount your deeds,
they will tell the glory of your might,
they will speak of the wonder of your power.

All shall hear of the marvels you have done,
of the splendour and glory of your reign;
for your kingdom is eternally a kingdom,
your dominion will endure evermore.

Our God is faithful when he speaks,
in all his works he is good;
he lifts up each soul in distress,
he raises up all who are down.

The eyes of all look to you in hope,
and you give in due time their food;
you open wide your hands
and satisfy their every desire.

The Lord is just in all his ways,
full of love in all that he does;
to those who call him he is near,
to all who invoke him in truth.

He supplies the needs of his friends,
he hears their cry and he saves,
the Lord keeps their souls in his love.

I will sing to the praise of the Lord:
let all flesh give thanks to his name,
he is holy, now, evermore!

Psalm 145 *(Heb. 146)*

Antiphon: At all times the Lord is true,
he gives justice to all the oppressed.

Praise the Lord, O my soul,
I will praise the Lord while I live,
I will sing for my God while I endure!

In the princes of men put no trust,
for no human strength can save;
their breath spent, they return to the dust,
on that day their plans are in vain.

Happy man if Jacob's God is your help,
if your hope is the Lord our God;
his hands made the heavens and the earth,
with the sea and all that it contains.

He keeps faith, at all times he is true,
he gives justice to all the oppressed;
he offers the hungry bread,
the Lord sets the captives free.

The Lord gives sight to the blind,
the Lord raises all who are down,
the stranger and the homeless he defends,
both orphans and widows he sustains.

The Lord loves all who are just,
but the plans of the wicked he thwarts;
for ever the Lord is king,
O Zion, your God evermore!

Psalm 146 *(Heb. 147A)*

Antiphon: He heals the broken in heart,
he binds up all their wounds.

Praise the Lord, it is good to sing praise!
Sing for our God, it is right to adore!

The Lord restores Jerusalem again,
he makes the exiles return;
he heals the broken in heart,
he binds up all their wounds;
he tells the number of the stars,
and he calls them each by their name.

Truly, great and almighty is our God,
to his wisdom there are no bounds,
the Lord lifts up the lowly,
the wicked he casts to the ground;
sing, give thanks to the Lord,
give praise on the harp to our God.

For he robes the heavens in clouds
and pours out rain for the earth;
on the mountains the grass springs up,
many plants for the service of men;
he gives to the cattle their food,
to the young of the ravens that cry.

He takes no delight in a horse,
the strength of our bodies he ignores;
his delight is in those who adore him,
with all who trust in his love.

Psalm 147 *(Heb. 147B)*

Antiphon: Give the glory to God, Jerusalem,
and worship the Lord, Zion, sing praise!

Give the glory to God, Jerusalem,
and worship the Lord, Zion, sing praise.

He has made strong the bars of your gates,
he has bless'd all who live within your walls;
he preserves the land in perfect peace,
you are nourished with the finest of wheat.

He gives his commands to the earth,
and all his words are quickly obeyed;
for the snow like a blanket he spreads,
and like dust he scatters the frost.

He hurls the hailstones of ice,
no one can stand the cold that he sends;
he commands, the snow melts away,
winds blow, the streams flow again.

To his people the Word was proclaimed,
to Israel, his laws and decrees;
what other lands did he treat in this way?
Not one ever heard his commands.

Psalm 148 *(Heb. 148)*

Antiphon: Glory to God in the highest,
and peace to his people on earth!

Praise the Lord in the heavens,
praise the Lord in the height;
praise the Lord, angel choirs,
praise the Lord, all his mighty hosts!

Praise the Lord, sun and moon,
praise the Lord, stars of light;
praise the Lord, highest heavens,
praise the Lord, heavenly waters high!

Let them praise the name of God,
he commanded and they stood;
he established evermore
a law which shall never fail.

Praise the Lord from the earth,
sea-creatures in the deep;
fire and hail, snow and mist,
storm and gale, you fulfil his word.

You mountains and all hills,
trees with fruit, cedars tall,
you creatures wild and tame,
crawling beasts, little birds that fly:

you kings and all mankind,
with the princes and the wise,
all girls and all young boys,
ancient heads and tiny babes:

praise the name of the Lord,
    for his glory is supreme
    and the splendour of his fame
rises far over all the earth.

He exalts his chosen race,
    he is praised by all the saints,
    he is bless'd in Israel's songs,
he is praised by his faithful friends.

Give glory to the Father
    and glory to the Son,
    give glory to the Spirit
now and evermore. Amen.

Psalm 149 *(Heb. 149)*

Antiphon: The Lord delights in his own,
with triumph the humble he arrays.

Now sing a new song to the Lord,
offer praise in the gathering of the saints;
in his Maker, let Israel be glad,
let Zion's children rejoice in their king!

Let them praise his name in the dance,
let them sing with cymbals and harps;
for the Lord delights in his own,
with triumph the humble he arrays.

In glory let the faithful exult,
let them sing for joy through the night,
all the praise of God on their lips,
for that is the glory of his friends!

Psalm 150 *(Heb. 150)*

Antiphon: Praise the Lord,
everything that lives!

Praise the Lord in the holiest of heights,
praise the Lord in his firmament of power,
praise the Lord for the wonder of his deeds,
praise the Lord, his glory is supreme!

Praise the Lord with a trumpet blast,
praise the Lord with the harp and the lyre,
praise the Lord with the strings and with flutes,
praise the Lord with dances and drums!

Praise the Lord, all cymbals resound!
Praise the Lord, loud cymbals resound!
Praise the Lord, everything that lives!
Praise the Lord! Praised be the Lord!

SINGING THE PSALMS

The Psalms were written to be sung. This present version was written with the singing-method of Father Gelineau in mind, a few of his melodies being included in this volume. However, it is also possible to have one or two soloists improvise on the words while the whole assembly regularly intervenes with some short chorus—for example, the Berthier canons so widely used by the people who know Taizé.

In each line of these Psalms there are a number of 'focal points'—usually 3, sometimes 2 or 4. It is the rhythmical progression of these 'points' that gives the musical structure. They should not be stressed unduly, although some emphasis is natural as the melodic line follows. The first word of a line is usually not one of these 'points', although it may be, while the final syllable of each line usually takes the value of a long note and is therefore the point of main emphasis. At times the final 'point' is a 'feminine' ending, the strong syllable being completed by a short weak one.

Parallelism is the basic structure of the Psalms, the old practice of dividing the assembly into two sections which alternate in reciting is a restful and meditative way of singing the longer texts. In this case, the usual division will be two lines, answered by two lines.

Antiphons

Antiphons, sung at the beginning and end of a Psalm, and after the *Gloria*, give a framework and expose either the theme of the Psalm or of the liturgical season. Antiphons for the liturgical year will be found at the end of this volume. The antiphons of most Psalms here are designed for use with the 'simple formulae', a single modulated line, which is usually preceded by a line in monotone. However, a certain number of antiphons are composed for the melodic antiphons which are part of the Gelineau system in its more developed form. It is hoped that it may be possible later to provide a musical edition of these antiphons, as well as a more complete musical system.

Simple Formulae

Any Psalm may be sung in unison following the treble voice of the following accompaniments. Each bar represents one line; in the case of 6 line Psalms, repeat the first two bars. In the case of 3 or 5 line groups, omit the penultimate bar. The Antiphon should be monotoned freely, pausing between the lines, up to the final cadence.

1.

2.

3.

4.

Melodic Formulae

These more melodic formulae may be sung in unison or in harmony by mixed voices. The first and second are for Psalms with regular lines of 3 'focal points'—the great majority—having 3, 4, 5 or 6 line sections. The first melody is more meditative, the second more joyful. The third formula is for 4 line sections with lines of 3 and 2 focal points alternating.

1. For 6 lines (for 5 lines omit section C; for 4 lines omit sections C & D; for 3 lines omit sections C, D & E)

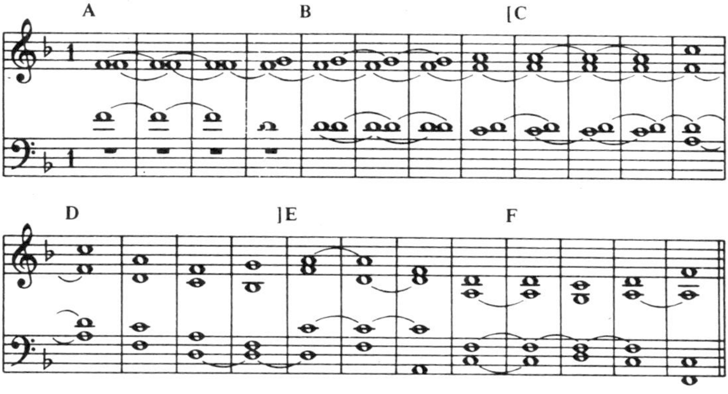

2. For 6 lines (*for 5 lines omit section E)

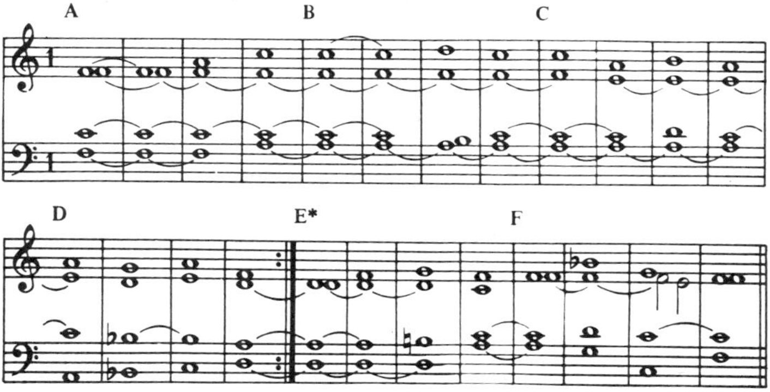

For 4 lines (*for 3 lines omit section B)

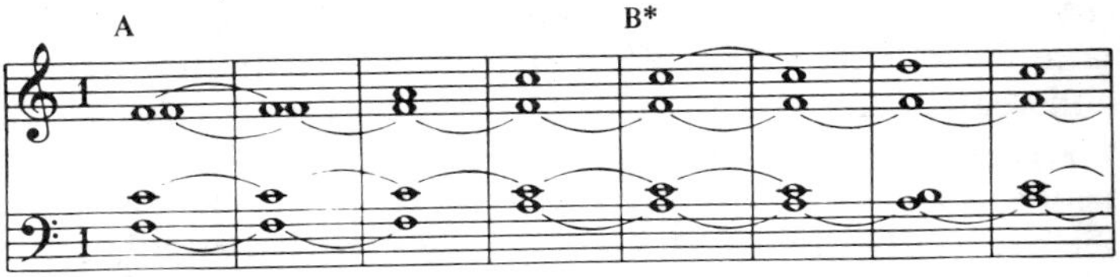

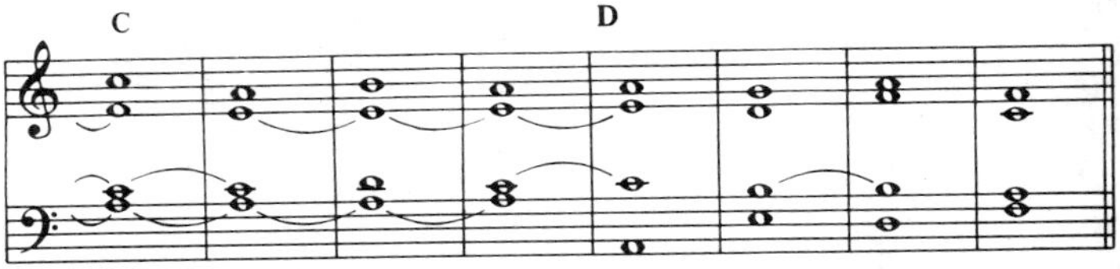

3. For 4 lines, 3+2 rhythm

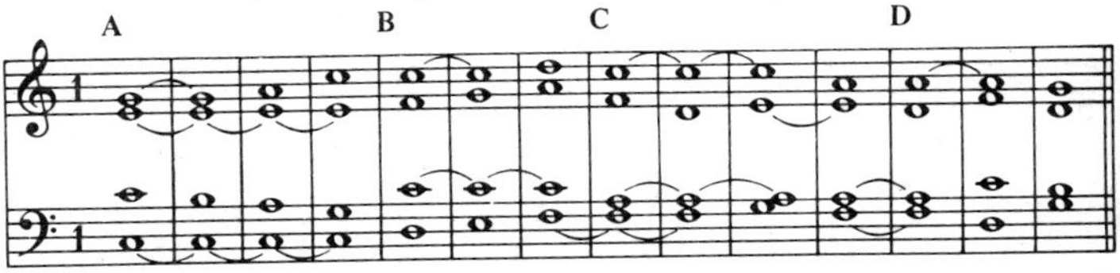

In the absence of special melodic antiphons, antiphons may be sung to the cadence of the last section of each formula.

N.B. The first note in each line of the melodic formulae is designed to cover the initial weak syllables coming before the first 'focal point' corresponding to the second note. In cases where there are no such weak syllables, this note is not sung, but it forms part of the accompaniment. It has no fixed value.

In Taizé we sing most of the Psalms to simple formulae, and only a small number to the melodic formulae which are more demanding of a strict rhythmic progression. People familiar with the ways of the Community at Taizé will find that they can sing each Psalm here in the way that it is sung at Taizé. Briefly, of the Melodic Formulae given here it can be said that Formula 1 is used for Psalms 1, 62, 91. Formula 2 for Psalms 8, 32, 94, 112, 134, 149 and 150. Formula 3 may be used for Psalms 41, 42, 64, 96 and 99. Of course, each formula may also be used to sing many other Psalms, but in some cases, since this is not a 'singing edition' and the 'focal points' are not marked, some experimentation will be required.

A SIX-WEEK COURSE OF PSALMS
(Septuagint/liturgical numbering)

		I	II	III	IV	V	VI
Sat.	pm	135	144	146	147	148	27
Sun.	am	91	96	98	145	149, 150	62
	pm	109, 110	111	113	114, 115	117	66
Mon.	am	118 I	118 III	118 V	118 VII	118 IX	49
	noon	118 II	118 IV	118 VI	118 VIII	118 X	83
	pm	1, 4	23	41	68 I	118 XI	92
Tues.	am	2, 3	24	44 I, 45	68 II	103 I	72
	noon	5	25	46	70	103 II	95
	pm	8	26	47	71	102	97
Wed.	am	6, 7	28, 29	50	74, 86	101	73
	noon	9	30 I	42	75	106 I	99
	pm	10, 12	30 II	54	76	106 II	112
Thur.	am	14, 16	31	53, 60	79	138	119, 120
	noon	15	32	55	80	139	121, 122
	pm	19, 20	33	61	84	140	123, 124
Fri.	am	21	35	56	87	128, 129	93
	noon	22	37	64	85	141	125–127
	pm	17 I	38	65	90	142	34
Sat.	am	17 II	39	67	88	136, 130	134
	noon	18	40	69	89	143	137

Evening prayers: Psalms 4, 90, 129
Night Vigils: Psalms 94, 97, 137
Psalm 100 may be used during Lent, Psalm 131 during Advent

If this list is used in conjuction with *Praise in all our Days—Common Prayer at Taizé*, the Psalms of week VI should be omitted during the Ordinary Days (Trinity to Advent, Epiphany to Lent) when many of them are used in the Introductions.

ANTIPHONS FOR THE LITURGICAL YEAR
(for use with any psalm)

Advent:	Almighty Lord, come and revive us, shine upon us and we shall be saved.
or:	Come, Lord, and visit us in peace.
Christmas:	The Word was made flesh and dwelt among us.
or:	This is the sign of the great King, salvation and peace for the world.
Epiphany:	The Magi worship the Child, the joy of the world is in him.
or:	All the ends of the earth have seen the salvation of our God.
Purification (Feb. 2):	Lord, now let your servant depart in peace.
Lent:	Return, O Lord, deliver my soul, save me for the sake of your love.
or:	Have pity on me, my strength is gone, Lord, how long till you return?
Holy Week:	Behold the Lamb of God, who takes away the sin of the world.
or:	Give light to my eyes, or they will close in death. (See also *Praise in all our Days—Common Prayer at Taizé*)

Easter:	Alleluia, alleluia!
or:	Christ is risen from the dead, the first of all who have fallen asleep.
Ascension:	Your love is high as the heavens, your faithfulness as the clouds.
Pentecost:	The Holy Spirit will teach you everything, He will lead you into all the truth.
or:	Come Holy Spirit, renew the face of the earth.
Trinity:	Holy, holy, holy, Lord God of heaven and earth.
or:	Let us worship and proclaim the wonder of the thrice-holy God.
Mary:	The Almighty chose her for his wonders, holy his name!
or:	You are bless'd among women, and bless'd is your child.
Saints:	Whoever shall confess the name of Jesus, God shall dwell in him and he in God.
or:	Their message covers the world, good news to the ends of the earth.
Transfiguration (Aug. 6):	In the shadow of the bright cloud, the glory of the living God!